TAKING
YOGA
OFF THE
MAT

Praise for *Taking Yoga Off the Mat*

A breath of fresh air. Lovely prose and optimism woven with reality.

As someone who guides people through the yoga experience, it is delightful to hear the reflections that follow the practice. Like the tender wet wings of a newly emerged butterfly, Jenni shares so honestly and beautifully through her delicately arranged words. "Taking Yoga Off the Mat" *is full of reality, delight, wit, and vulnerability—sprinkled with images that speak poetically themselves.*

Day-to-day events are presented bravely with raw honesty and interwoven with yogic teaching, inviting you to take on all of life and open your inner heart as you reflect on your own experiences.

— SUZANNE GOSSETT AWAN, Yoga Shelter Instructor & Wellness Coach

"Taking Yoga Off the Mat" *is a contemplative view into the practical uses of this ancient physical discipline. Jenni is an inspirational storyteller who shares with us her continued yoga journey and its daily uses in her personal, professional, social, and spiritual life. Yoga practitioner or still thinking about it, this is a must read for anyone aspiring to be more present in the moment.*

— JERRY NEHR, Author of *Erasing the Margins*

While you and I may not practice yoga, each of us have a 'mat' of our own where we find our certainty, validation, and self-love. Mine is swimming, from my earliest childhood, where I have always found peace, swimming down to the deep end when I could finally find my solace, my inner voice, and my answers. Reading Jenni Carmichael Clark's "Taking Yoga Off the Mat" *is so inspirational, it gave me the strength to jump into the deep end of my own self-discovery.*

— EILEEN KENT, President, Custom Keynotes, LLC

An inspiring personal journey for all busy yoga lovers! Jenni Carmichael Clark shows us how to find the peace of yoga wherever we are.

— ED NAHHAT, Founder of Shakespeare Royal Oak

TAKING

YOGA

OFF THE

MAT

Thoughts & Essays

JENNI CARMICHAEL CLARK

Triumph Press is a resource for those who have the passion to tell their life-stories and change the world. If you have a true and inspiring story to share, visit
www.TrimphPress.com

Dedication

for Jarod and Paige

You have been writing your own stories since your earliest moments on this earth. As you continue your adventures, remember that before Alice reached Wonderland, she had to fall pretty hard down a deep rabbit hole. Anything can happen if you believe in yourself— and at least six impossible things— nurture courage and curiosity, and just do the work.

Gratitude

What is the Intent of your Practice today? I cannot tell you how many times I have heard that question. Most yoga classes begin with that query. An "intention" guides the mind, provides a focal point for thoughts, and fundamentally supports the whole yoga practice. Answers and "intentions" vary based on where a yogi *IS* at that moment, what is happening in their life, and what thoughts are swirling around their mind. But fundamentally, an intention provides a grounding chord and directs the work.

My intention at this moment is to express gratitude. No creative project like this happens without others crossing your path to effect it. I feel an incredible sense of appreciation for the people who encouraged, supported, and helped me take an idea from my head, shape it with my heart, a blue .5 Uniball pen and a pokey pencil, and form it into the words you see before you now.

My teachers from the Detroit area Yoga Shelter offered the groundwork that gave breath to this creative endeavor. Much appreciation to Yoga Shelter, especially my "home" studio in downtown Royal Oak. Thank you to Marty, Brittney, Matt (*oh how I miss the three of you!*) and Stephanie. Special gratitude to Emily, your joy and effervescent energy bubbles forth and has brightened many a dark moment. And Suzanne, your classes are therapy to my soul. You help me to ground and walk my path with mindfulness and grace.

Judy Lebryk—the most challenging English teacher at Valparaiso High School—thank you for introducing me to Jane Austen and the Greek and Roman myths and for never accepting less than my best.

To Gloria Zimmerman, *who knew the impact VHS' 1983-84 Valenian class would have on my writing?* "You gotta have a gimmick" may have originated with a Broadway musical, but it was also a creative writing technique I learned in your classroom. I've been applying it ever since.

Eileen Kent, you helped light my way to "The Corner." Thank you for encouraging me to open the door to that place of discovery—and for always reading, listening, and helping me find the courage to keep my "little light" shining.

Dick Cheatham, you told stories like no one I know—guiding me to embark on an incredible walk of discovery, faith, and spirituality. And you read everything I wrote until the day you left these mortal coils to begin your next great adventure. I will always value your thoughtful words and your incredible capacity to keep learning. I treasure the time we shared.

Doug Clark, thank you for believing in me and encouraging me, my work, my writing, my yoga, my dreams, my passions, and my Madness too! You continuously support me and my introverted need for time and space to write and explore. I love you for that and so much more.

Jarod and Paige. You inspire me daily, sharing your sunshine and starlight, and empowering me to cultivate my own inner strength to tether myself on and off the mat. Thank you for allowing me to be part of your narratives and play a role in the stories you are still writing—and for encouraging me to find the words to shape mine.

Ellie. I didn't truly know I was a "cat" person until you found me. How many times you have joined me on my mat, your purrs of contentment as grounding as any meditation or pose. You help me believe in the magnitude of unconditional love. Thank you for every single moment.

Mom and Dad, you taught me to believe in myself and to do the work. You encouraged me to dream and to hang in there when things went wonky. Thank you for *always* being there for me during the amazing, the good, the not so good, the bloody awful, and the landing on the moon incredible times. I love you.

And to my Heavenly Father, you bless my life with words—and so much more—and walk by my side day by day.

So many others have traveled with me on this transformative journey, helping shape these essays. Some of you moved my soul to dance and stayed around. Some of you moved on, lost to time and distance, but leaving unique, indelible footprints on my heart. Special thanks to Jeff & Marcy Carmichael, Mandy Reinke, Cheryl Comeau, Abby & Chris Carmichael, Jack & Gloria

Clark, Joe Donovan, Caitlin Bringardner, Molly Donovan, Maura Polack, Jerry Nehr, Lauren McVean & the Beach House, Matthew Troyer, Joseph Magee, Ed Nahhat, Holly Conroy, Kathleen Lietz, Kevin Branshaw, Doc O, Alice Gambel, Shelly Kemp, and Jeff Nelson. Thank you for your support, love, guidance, and friendship. Thank you for moments you probably don't even realize you gave me—and for long walks and laughter; conversations over cocktails or coffee; beach-side sunsets, mountain hikes, and theatre highlight reels; and everything in between.

Thanks to Melanie and Triumph Press for enthusiastically saying "Yes" to my project, making my dream to publish this book come true.

And you dear reader, thank you for reading. I hope my words instill in you a sense of mindfulness, guiding you to take your yoga off the mat—whatever that means for you.

Alice in Wonderland has always intrigued me. She was a curious, adventurous soul—and, like me, a little Mad, since all the best people are. Lewis Carroll's wisdom may seem like nonsense to some, but to me it resonates quite clearly. As the Mad Hatter once said:

*"The secret, Alice, is to surround yourself with people
who make your heart smile. It's then, only then,
you'll find Wonderland."*

*And He said to them, "Come aside
by yourself to a deserted place
and rest awhile."*
— **Mark 6:31**

*"Sometimes I believe in as many as
Six Impossible Things before breakfast."*
— **Alice in Wonderland**

Author's Note

A standard yoga mat is 68 inches long, 24 inches wide, and approximately 3/16 of an inch thick. Yet this mat is the essential tool for students of yoga to ground, stretch, and strengthen their bodies, as well as tone their minds and spirits.

Students of yoga go through so much on these mats. During a typical 60— to 90—minute yoga class, students— typically referred to as "yogis"— are challenged to first quiet their minds and find stillness in their bodies, focusing solely on their breath. Then, they are guided to move through a series of quite challenging poses and flows which ask them to both reach high and bend low— two very opposite demands, at the exact same time. Then come the balancing poses—varying from one leg and arm in the air to handstands and taking flight. And at long last, there are stretches and a final resting, meditation pose called Savasana. And during all this, the true focus remains on the breath: Just Keep Breathing.

If we can handle all of this *ON* the mat, then we have within us all we need to draw on the strength, the quiet mind, and the recognition that we are still okay—even when we fall over or can't do a "pose"—when we move *OFF* the mat.

If we can do hard things *ON* the mat, then we can also do hard things when we move *OFF*. To do so, though, we need to apply the skills, mantras, and concepts we practice in class when we leave the yoga studio—or when we leave our homes, offices, etc. Our bodies can make it through complex, unpredictable flows in a warm yoga studio without losing its cool. So, with a little practice, we can learn to cultivate this same strength within our minds and bodies to make it through complex, difficult, challenging, unpredictable days, weeks, months, and even years!

I can be playful on my mat, so I can learn to find my playful side when I roll it up. I can find strength and courage during a flow, so I can learn to "flow with it, baby" when I am off the mat, calling on that same strength and courage. I can be adventurous and daring, experimenting, and trying new things without judgment on the mat. So, I can practice what I've learned there and do the same when I am facing something new and unexpected in the "real world."

Learning to accept myself for who I am on the mat transitions to embracing the authentic, imperfect yet amazing me *OFF* the mat.

No matter what type of exercise regime you pursue—yoga, running, weightlifting, swimming, basketball, skating, dance, etc.—you are challenged to maintain breath and a clear mind when you are in the midst of it. Exercise creates endorphins—natural "feel good" body chemicals that help us cope with pain and stress, making us both mentally and physically stronger in the process. Even if actual "exercise" isn't your "jam," merely walking outside and simple day-to-day movement supports your mental health and physical body. But when we wrap it up, shower, and move on with our day, all that clarity of thinking tends to fall to the wayside. When we get in the car to head home from class and someone cuts us off on the road, all that "calm" gets lost, as we pound our horn and rage about some driver who probably dismissed us from his mind within seconds of the offending behavior.

I am a curious soul—a seeker, adventurer, and writer for as long as I can remember. I live in a world that constantly complicates the idea of existence, achieving success, and finding joy. See, I believe that we learn as much from the times we cannot hold a pose in a yoga class as we do from the times the flows come easy. Just because it is smooth postures one day does not mean we will not encounter a disturbance the next time we climb onto our mat. The key, then, becomes the choices we make, the forgiveness and grace we offer ourselves when we struggle with perfectionism, and the acceptance we embrace to actualize true contentment.

So, in the following pages, I am offering exercises to help you take yoga off the mat. Exercises to find calm in the midst of chaos and draw on strength of mind and stamina of body. All the while, remembering to *Just Keep Breathing.*

Contents

INTRODUCTION

I have been writing for as long as I can remember. Encouraged by two friends a few years back, I started to share some of my essays publicly on a blog to inspire others. After reading some of these blogs a few years back, my son Jarod told me that I should write a book. He said I should call it "Listen to Me: I Know What I'm Talking About ... "

"Because..." he explained in his simple pre-teen tone. "You do."

Since that initial suggestion, I have learned—the hard way at times—that I do not always know what I am talking about. I have even had more than a few heated discussions about that very concept with both of my kids over the years. That said, I must begin with a disclaimer that in these pages I will offer my best thoughts—imperfect, emotionally charged, and heartfelt as they might be. As you read, I encourage you to take what resonates with you and then let go of the rest.

My son is now an adult, and my daughter is firmly established into her teenage years. While they were growing up, I continued to write, sharing my thoughts, perspectives, and philosophy for them and anyone else who cared to read my words in a blog called *My Own Little Corner by Jenni* (myownlittlecornerbyjenni.wordpress.com). It was inspired by the Rodgers & Hammerstein song from the musical Cinderella, "In My Own Little Corner," which reinforced the idea that when I write, I can be whatever I want to be. I can say whatever I want to say. I can dream, imagine, create, discover, and explore too.

So now comes the time to actually do something with those years of reflective, questioning essays. Now is the time to stitch them together and see if anyone out there might be curious or adventurous enough to read these thoughts from the corner, connecting my prose into their own lives.

Many of these chapters began their formation when I was on my yoga mat—either during a yoga class, during pre-class meditations, or as I walked back into the world after a session. It is during these moments that my heart and mind are most open and ready to be vulnerable, authentic, and quiet. I learn so much as I attempt to balance on one leg or breathe into a difficult pose. I give that still, small voice a chance to be heard.

On the mat, I feel strong, safe, supported, and completely myself. I am not competitive, nor do I waste time comparing myself with someone else. I am compassionate with myself, open to the guidance and wisdom offered by others, and both curious and courageous when it comes to the unexpected challenge coming my way.

I have been known to laugh on my mat, wave with my foot during the difficult Half-Moon pose, curse, mutter, and even shed more than a few tears. In that space, I feel and, perhaps just as importantly, I give myself grace and permission to just "be." I release judgment.

Now, I recognize that you, dear reader, may not have any interest in yoga or even exercise at all. That is absolutely fine. In these pages, I have taken those times on the mat and pondered the questions:

- *How can I take all this—this real, authentic, imperfect, kind, reflective, courageous self-discovery OFF the mat?*

- *How does this yoga philosophy reach out and touch real life... and day to day "stuff?"*
- *How can I nurture the version of me I create during yoga-time to find peace, grounding, compassion, acceptance, and a new view of all that is happening around me and to me in the "real" world?*

Those are my questions, and these are the questions I'd like you to consider as you read on, answering them for yourself. And–good news–I am doing all the yoga for you. The chapters in this little book offer some thoughts on doing just that—taking yoga OFF the mat and INTO the world.

Namaste,
Jenni

Namaste is a Sanskrit phrase shared at the end of a yoga class. It can be translated in many ways. Typically, it means "I bow to you" or "I honor the light in you." For my purposes, I connect Namaste to the following phrase learned from many of my own yogis (that is, yoga teachers) at Yoga Shelter: "The divine light in me honors the divine light in you... because it is the same."

Fundamentally, when a yoga practice ends and the class utters "Namaste" together, it is a message that celebrates and honors the highest, truest, most authentic parts of themselves–connecting them to one another and giving them the mental and physical strength to allow limitations and self-judgment to fall away as they walk out the door and return to their daily lives.

Everything I Need to Know
I Learned in Yoga

"Offer your best and let go of the rest."
—Marty Time

D o you remember that Robert Fulghum book, *Everything I Need to Know I Learned in Kindergarten?* I have a well-worn copy on my bookshelf. One day, as I rolled up my mat after a much-needed yoga session, I realized the same principles applied—that *EVERYTHING* I needed to know, I learned in yoga.

To be honest, I began my yoga journey on a bit of a lark. As a child, my family followed the football season of The Dallas Cowboys. Odd, I guess, for a girl growing up in Northern Indiana. But we had family in Texas, so it connected us. One day, as I browsed fitness DVDs looking for something new for my workout regime, I ran across "The Dallas Cowboy Cheerleaders Yoga" program. I had to buy it.

The very first time I played it, I realized yoga was more than a fitness program and this DVD was not a joke. The Instructor, Kurt Johnsen, guided the poses while offering more than the encouraging "you can do it" fitness banter I heard during aerobics sessions. His words engaged my mind, body, and spirit in a completely new way. As someone with a workout habit that began at age 12 with Jane Fonda, that was saying something. I realized that if I embraced it fully, yoga would soften the edges around my busy mind, while it strengthened my body and spirit.

Flash-back a few years and pregnant me—who did not want to sacrifice 26 years of exercise to the whims of the developing offspring inside—discovered prenatal yoga. More than a "fitness program for pregnant women," the program offered a unique perspective on wellness. I found myself embracing both the moves and the ideas, becoming increasing confident that I could do this crazy delivery thing and stay physically fit in the process.

The class' messaging reinforced that I was strong enough to do difficult things and trained both my body and mind to handle what was coming my way.

So, a few years later when my doctor suggested yoga as a way of managing my anxiety, I bought a Groupon and headed to my first actual, non-video yoga class at *Yoga Shelter* in Royal Oak, Michigan. That was nearly 10 years ago.

Since that time, I have learned more than how to do poses. I have come to understand that yoga does more than tone my body. It tones my mind and spirit. What I take *OFF* the mat at the *end* of class is as significant as what I do *ON* the mat during class.

Whether you do yoga or not, I know you can improve your life through the principles I have learned in my practice. Here is a list:

1. Offer your best and let go of the rest.

2. You can do hard things.

3. No matter how challenging the pose is, the difficult moment will end. Really!

4. That difficult moment really IS only a moment. It may seem like forever in the middle of the night, when worries dance around your head like crazy monkeys or when you are trying to make it thru chair pose and your legs are shaking so hard you do not know how you can hold it one more second. Yes, it seems like an eternity. But that really hard pose—that extremely difficult "whatever" that is making you struggle and anxious—truly lasts only a moment.

5. Be yourself. Do your yoga. No one is looking at you and comparing their half- moon pose to yours. Seriously, they are just trying to hold the balance themselves!

6. Child's pose is always an option. Retreat. Restore. Modulate. No one will judge you for that. A yoga mat is 24" x 68". It is your safe space. What you do there is about you and no one else.

7. Breathe... that is really what yoga is about. Maintaining your breath and your calm is the work. No matter what comes your way, what pose is thrown at you, what challenge you encounter, or what difficulty sends your spirit reeling... just Breathe.

8. Balancing is difficult. Balancing is really frickin' hard. On the mat. Off the mat.

9. It's okay if you fall. Just get back on your feet and try again. Do not give up. Go ahead and take child's pose until you are ready to try again. That's okay too. Offer yourself grace.

10. Accept yourself and what you offer. You are the best you. Release judgment of yourself and you may just discover how to stop judging others.

12. Be present. Now is all you really have. Stop living in the past. Stop worrying about the future.

12. Close your eyes. Release. Let it go. Yes, you can.

13. Shaking in a pose is just your body requesting strength.

14. If it hurts or causes you to lose it, do not do the pose. Getting upset because of a yoga pose is not worth it. Getting upset because of _____ (*fill in the blank*) is also not worth it. You can't control other people or situations. All you can control is how you respond to them.

15. You never really know what is coming next. Each class—each hour, day, week, etc., brings the unknown. You may think you know what is next in the flow of life, but you really cannot predict it. All you can do is Breathe and take one pose at a time.

16. Know your truth. Honor who you are. It really is enough.

17. The real yoga begins when you walk out the door.

I don't know whether or not you do yoga—or if an exercise program plays any part in your life. I'm not suggesting yoga is the answer for everyone. But these things I have learned, they come off the mat, too. They have altered the way I see things, the way I see others, the way I react to situations, and the way I see myself.

So, I attend yoga classes—both virtual and live sessions in this current world environment. And, when I sit down on the mat at the very beginning to ground and meditate, I remember that all I really must do is Breathe. I don't know what is coming next there, any more than I know what is coming next in the "real world." Just when I settle into Triangle pose, Majorette or Airplane challenges come my way. My legs are shaking; I am sweating, and I am trying to stay calm. I wobble... I even fall sometimes. But I am learning to listen and recognize what each "pose" is teaching me. In those moments on the mat, I am finding my own strength. I am finding new ways to embrace calm, no matter what "flow" comes at me.

And I take *THAT* off the mat and out the door.

Make Me A Mix Tape

"Music washes away from the soul
the dust of everyday life."
—Bertold Auerbach

O ne of the first elements of yoga that I noticed when I entered the studio was music. In fact, it was the music that I first focused on during class. The songs playing during the hour on my mat drew my attention away from the fidgets when a pose was difficult or needed to be held longer than my muscles wished.

I remember focusing on a specific song that resonated with me—on its lyrics and what they said to me personally. I often found myself reciting the chorus or specific verse over and over in my mind, hoping I might recall just enough of the song to download it to my Apple Music account when class ended. I felt certain that if I listened to those specific songs that touched my spirit *in the room*, they would help me recapture the calm state achieved there, even when I was away from the studio.

I created numerous playlists in an effort to recapture that feeling. Music helped transform my mood and mind, reminding me of words or messages uttered during class. But then, music has also spoken to me and "soothed the savage beast" on days when nothing else would.

I fondly recall making "Mix Tapes" as a teenager. Pardon me while I date myself, but there was something neat about selecting the music from one tape and transferring it with the push of a few buttons to record a compilation of songs on the second tape. I had several favorites and played them until they ran thin, or broke.

The Mix Tape creation practice was methodical and fun. I painstakingly selected songs that I enjoyed—songs that I wanted to share with a friend, songs that held special meaning, or songs that presented a particular message—and

gathered the different tapes together to create that one special Mix Tape. The first song to play was key... and then the final song anchored the message. Because, for me, music has always held meaning. And creating a Mix Tape was like writing a letter or poem for someone I cared enough about to invest this crazy amount of time and effort.

The challenge with the Mix Tape was timing.

I mean, you had to get it right or the tape would cut off a song or end too abruptly. More than once I would get to the end of a tape and it would cut off early in the midst of the anchor song, forcing me to start all over to get the timing—and the complete message— right.

The days of the Mix Tape are long gone. Cars no longer even come with tape decks. If you can find a stereo system that has one—or a tape-to-tape "boom box"—you would be hard pressed to actually find a tape to put inside. Oh, I have one—a blank tape. A friend of mine found one in his possession a few years ago. I keep it, more out of sentimentality than anything else. The Mix Tape started something that survives today though, just under a new name.

Now we make "Playlists" and have unlimited access to songs through music streaming services. I have Apple Music. My kids prefer Spotify. And they make their own mix tapes— okay, playlists. They make playlists for long car rides or trips, playlists of the month, playlists to exercise or to study by—you get the gist. So, the tradition of the Mix Tape carries on to the next generation, just with a seamless format.

My kids make me Mix Tapes/Playlists. For the past two years, my Mother's Day gift from my daughter has been a specially cultivated Apple Music Playlist that she "gifts" to me in a text. I download it to my phone and listen to her narrative. Some songs are dedications. Some songs tell me the music that connects to her spirit. Whatever the case, it is something meaningful we share. And, as I take long walks or drive around town, the music speaks volumes about what matters to Paige and what musical dialogue supports her soul. In these playlists, the first and final song seem to have special meaning to her— just like the ones I created once upon a time.

A yoga class flows similarly to my old Mix Tape process. The early moments of music set the tone and help you settle on your mat. Then the music and the class build up to support your breath as you stretch. The early flows help your body become stronger and your mind focus so you can prepare for the more challenging poses that eventually come your way.

The music at the beginning of class tends to be quieter, more reflective. Then, as the momentum picks up, so do the beats and rhythms of the musical selections. Several instructors even turn up the volume during more challenging core or strengthening moments. At first, the heightened volume confused me. But then I discovered that it gave me something to focus on when the flowing got tough. Ingenious, right?

When yoga (or life) gets challenging, we can pump up the volume so the music can support mind, body, and spirit. Music does that on the mat, and it does it off the mat, too.

During the Covid-19 quarantine when yoga classes went virtual, the significance of the class playlist became even more apparent. Instructors would count down so the class could press "play" on the provided Spotify playlist at the exact same moment. Poses and flows were enhanced by these musical selections. It was crystal clear that certain songs were chosen to support that practice.

Unfortunately, I have Apple Music, so I don't have a Premium Spotify account. I can still use the playlists provided for the class, but the songs play out of sequence and are interrupted by commercials, which tends to disrupt the yoga mood and push me out of the flow. My virtual yoga classes take place music-free, and in those moments on the mat without music, I find it much more difficult to keep my mind from rushing off to places dark, busy, and distracting.

Ever since I can remember, music has been a source of happiness, peace, and joy. During the pandemic, I listened to a lot of Josh Groban, attending his six virtual concerts. His music nurtured and uplifted my moods in a time when life was just hard and the next pose in my "flow" unpredictable.

"Music does more than soothe the soul,
it brings balance to the mind, body, and spirit."
—Bertice Berry

I don't listen to music in a yoga class the same way I did in the beginning of my practice, but I hear it. It resonates deep inside. Music speaks in a language all its own with rhythms and lyrics that mute my busy mind on and off the mat.

My Sock Drawer is Messy

"Strive for Progress, not Perfection."
—every teacher at *Yoga Shelter*

I don't live in Perfect.
But I don't live in Good Enough, either.

Somewhere along the way—in my formative years—I inherited my Dad's neat-nick habits. Everything has a place and there is a place for everything. I like and maintain a *neat and clean* car, *a neat and clean* desk, *a neat and clean* house, *a neat and clean* kitchen, a *neat and clean* refrigerator, *and neat and clean* cabinets.

Neat and clean. See? There is a theme here.

I clean my home weekly. I appreciate vacuum lines on my carpet and non-sticky floors. Dust makes me nuts. Counters are wiped down regularly, and bathroom mirrors are streak free. We have a cat, so making sure the litter box area is swept up and cat hair is vacuumed supports my sanity.

During my workout this afternoon, though, one of my favorite fitness gurus, Jillian Michaels, mentioned that there are those of us who are too obsessed with "being perfect." We are hard on ourselves when things go awry or do not play out in that nice, structured way we have planned. We are critical of our looks, our bodies, our weight, our homes, our lives, our friends, our performance, our significant others... and so on. And that criticism holds us back. Makes us give up too quickly. It keeps our minds, spirits, bodies, and even our relationships from achieving their personal potential.

We are focused on something that cannot be achieved. Perfection.

Well, I don't live in perfect. And as neat as my home is, there are still places where it's just plain messy... where I am messy. And when I look too closely at those places, I can make myself crazy.

I attend yoga and Barre3 classes daily. I do Jillian Michaels videos as well, trying my best to achieve toned arms and that super flat stomach that I know I can have if I just work hard enough. But I'm not there. Yet. So, I keep working out. It's a process. When I'm doing jumps or lunges, my breath comes quicker, and my heartbeat races. And I've been working out daily for over...well, let's not talk age, okay? Let's just leave it at this: I've been working out for a really long time. I'm in shape, but not Jillian Michaels shape.

Exercising supports my mind and my spirit. It supports my health and my body. But, if you think I am going to give up the occasional beer, basket of fries, Milky Way bar, or delectable slice of chocolate cake to achieve that super flat belly, well... not going to happen.

'Cause, I don't live in perfect.

I guess that is another reason why I am drawn to yoga. Yoga is not billed as an exercise. It's a practice. I practice yoga. I don't perfect it. And I don't strive to be perfect when I am on my mat. There are times I have lost my balance. Times I have literally fallen over. There are poses I just can't do. Period. I've yet to do a handstand or stick my leg straight out and grab my toes. I may never be able to hold crow pose on my arms for longer than a moment before I fall on my face. (Trust me—that's a real thing that I've done.) I may hop about before I land myself firmly in King Dancer. But I can still practice. I can still try. And no one kicks me out of a yoga class if I don't do a pose like they do—or if I choose to do something different than what the instructor calls out.

> *"The thing that is really hard and really amazing is giving up on being perfect and beginning the work on becoming yourself."*
> —Anna Quindlen

Yoga... the Firm workouts... Barre3... Jane Fonda... Kettlebell Circuit Training... and even long walks, each of these workouts help me align my body, my mind, and my spirit. I will never master them. Some days on my mat are better than others. Some days I trip on a root or a bump on a sidewalk just taking a simple walk around the neighborhood. A weight is too heavy, or I don't make a smooth transition on my mat. It's no different from days at work. There are just some projects on my desk that are neater, stronger, better organized, or more structured than others.

Some relationships in my life are messier or more challenging or more inspiring on any given day. Some experiences are bumpier. Some people are difficult or unpredictable.

And... there are times I spill popcorn in a movie theatre. I admit it, and I sincerely apologize to whoever ended up having to clean up my mess. I tried to pick up as much as I could, really. But, well, we do not live in perfect. We are all works in progress. We do our best at any given moment. And to place the pressure of perfection on any aspect of our lives is to court certain doom.

However, I also do not live in Good Enough. I can't look at a relationship or a project and be satisfied if I do not offer my best. I can let go when I know I have done all I can. I have accepted that there are some things beyond my control. Some people with whom a relationship is too difficult, some projects that may never be completed, some dust under the bed I cannot reach... a drawer full of socks that never seems to stay organized no matter how many times I dump it on the floor and reorder it.

But if I *know* I have offered my best... that's all I need to do. And then be brave enough to let go.

No, I don't and never will live in Perfect. I fall on and off my mat. It's part of my journey. As neat, put together, and organized as I may seem, there are places in my life that are just plain messy.

Like my sock drawer.

I'm okay with that. Jillian accepts me as I am. So does my family and those I count as my truest friends.

My yoga instructors support me and guide me along, even with my imperfections. Each time I come to my mat, I work out, and I work in. Heck, that's what I do daily. I wouldn't want to change that... I am still a work in progress.

And if what I offer is not good enough for someone, well, they can move to Perfect and leave me be.

The Start of Something: "No"

"As I look back on my life, I realize that every time I thought I was being rejected from something good, I was actually being re-directed to something better."
—Steven Maraboli

No, you didn't get the job.

No, you didn't get that role.

No, you didn't do that right.

No, you need to come up with a different approach.

No, I can't see you anymore.

No, it's not good enough.

Recently, my son went off to college. So much of the previous year had been wrapped up in his senior year activities, ceremonies, events, and "lasts." Packing him off to school was an adventure—and kind of emotional for me. It left an empty bedroom and a quieter calendar.

So, I had time on my hands. And since I am a restless spirit that likes to be physically, mentally, and emotionally active, I don't sit still very well... or very long.

I had an idea about how to fill those hours—a theatre project that would present me with a new challenge and a more active schedule. I tossed my hat into the ring. Sometimes, though, the answer is not yes, and our best laid plans don't come to fruition. It's not necessarily a good or bad thing. It's just what it is. And as humans, when we encounter a stop or a detour sign, we tend to struggle a bit and question our place in the grand scheme. We doubt our skills or our talents. We might get emotional and rage or cry for a while, mourning the loss.

Then, we just have to dust off our egos and figure out what to do next.

In the midst of it, I stumbled upon a quote I wrote down once upon a time: *"As I look back on my life, I realize that every time I thought I was being rejected from something good, I was actually being re-directed to something better."* — Steven Maraboli

How many transformative opportunities in my life—or in your life—have begun with the word "No?" Perhaps you applied for a job, but it didn't materialize. I recall wanting a particular job SO BADLY. The application process was delayed, and another interview came through, landing me an offer. I debated... should I hold out for something I thought I wanted that *might* come through or trust this new, unexpected opportunity, and move forward?

Answer? I closed my eyes and jumped. And my time in that job as Marketing Coordinator with Magic Line, Inc. was seriously the greatest six years in my career. It was a time of growth, learning, discovery, accomplishment, success, and joy. I planned an event at the Palmer House Hilton in Chicago, for goodness' sake! (I grew up outside Chicago where the Palmer House was "THE" classic Chicago hotel. So that was a HUGE thing for me.) Anyway, that position and my time there shaped my entire career, and I am forever grateful that I said "yes" to that opportunity.

So back to the earlier comment about filling my hours with a theatre project when my son went off to college. I auditioned for this play. I thought it was a good fit, and I went prepared. But... I didn't get the part. A friend of mine was cast instead. As we drank beers and ate truffle fries together after the "casting call," I remember a few tears of disappointment slipping out. But there was another show and another role that I had been preparing for at the time as well... two great shows with great roles auditioning only a week apart.

The other show intrigued me. And, after I shook off the "no" from the week prior, I brought my A-game to that competitive, challenging audition. Something clicked for me there, in those moments. Two tough days of auditions and a brutal call-back later, and I got the part. I can honestly admit, I had an incredible time in that production of *Don't Dress for Dinner*. Moral of the story? I am as grateful for the initial "no" as I am for the eventual "yes"— and the friendships that evolved with my director and the exceptionally talented cast.

The "no's" will come. They will come in various forms and ways. Sometimes they are presented in a kind, understanding manner. Sometimes they are delivered crisply over the phone or by text, letter, or email. Sometimes they come face-to-face. Sometimes they occur in the silence of an unreturned phone call or message. Sometimes you lose a job or a relationship. Sometimes you don't understand what happened or what you didn't do. Sometimes you want to ask questions, but you are stopped short. Sometimes you just never understand the "why."

But you have to go on. The Rolling Stones got it. Remember the message in their classic hit? *"You can't always get what you want. But if you try sometimes... you just might find... you get what you need."*

Sometimes it takes a "no" to propel us forward. Sometimes the "no" gets us to the next better thing... or to the right thing seven things down from that one. It's not always formulaic, and it doesn't always happen immediately or in our preferred timing. The door closes and, from time to time, the window can remain stuck and keep you stuck there with it.

But we learn from "no." We evolve from "no." We grow sad and strong from "no." We mourn, and we lament when we get a "no." We rant and rave as well. But we change from "no." A dead end is a dead end. We have to turn onto a new path when one road closes. We cannot just stop and curl into the fetal position. Well, okay, we can. I have. But we can only linger in that fetal position for a little while.

"When you stop chasing the wrong things,
you give the right things a chance to catch you."
—Lolly Daskal

Life is full of "yes." Life is full of "no." And sometimes to get to a "yes," you have to experience a whole lot of "no."

I like to think—I choose to believe—that each "no" presents an opportunity for growth and a gentle push onto a different path, a path that I might not have chosen had I received the word "yes." I need both in my life to become the best *ME* I can be. I may not always like to get them, but a "no" is necessary to shape my character and help me simmer for a while to make me stronger, to help me find the next right thing.

With a "no," my life does not end. I am not broken, destroyed, lost, or set out to sea. My path is simply re-routed, redirecting me to something different... something... New!

Find Your Focal Point

"The secret to life is to put yourself in the right lighting."
—Susan Cain

G rowing up, I took ballet—like many little girls do, I suppose. My parents agreed it would be both good exercise and good for my posture. Secretly, as I practiced at the ballet barre my dad installed in our basement, I dreamed of the time I would be selected to be fitted in those elegant pink satin toe shoes and a tutu. I looked forward to the day I would dance "on pointe," spinning and leaping across the stage in front of an enraptured audience in some dazzling production crafted by a Russian composer.

Unfortunately, that was one childhood fantasy doomed to failure. During ballet classes, I was terrible at "spotting," which was key to learning to spin successfully across the dance floor without losing your balance.

Posture, I got. Pointe shoes, I did not.

To keep my balance, I needed to find and maintain a focal point. Nearly 40 years after my last ballet class, I am still learning to how to choose a focal point that keeps me from falling to the floor.

"Decide what you want. Declare it to the world.
See yourself winning. And remember that if you are
persistent as well as patient, you can get whatever you seek."
—Misty Copeland

A few years ago, I took on the role of Social Chair for a local community theatre. My end- of-the-season and most daunting project was to coordinate a black-tie gala, a celebratory Tony Awards-like event. And Event Planner that I am, I wanted to make it special. The location I had selected was elegant. Every attendee was dressed to the nines. The menu was excellent. The décor was sensational. I had reviewed and triple-checked every detail. The evening's hosts and entertainment offered surprises that elicited laughter, a few poignant tears, and clever camaraderie. The ballroom and flowers on each table were beautiful. Happy energy flowed as friends reconnected, smiled, danced, and socialized throughout the evening. All in all, it was an exceptional seven hours!

So why, in the morning light, did I find myself thinking about what went wrong during the evening? Why was my mind dwelling on that handful of critical comments and complaints? Why did my attention turn so quickly to the imperfections and flaws?

Spotlight in my role as GPT Clarence Banquet Social Chair Photo by David Reed

Let me say, too, that I looked amazing. Great dress, jewelry, nails, hair, and shoes. The footwear is key. And the sparkly black/silver fishnet hose added just the right dramatic flair. I felt like I walked on air. I was centered, grounded, and completely calm. Not stressed. Ready. (I took a yoga class that morning to get myself in the right frame of mind for the day.)

Did I mention that I looked amazing?

The evening rolled out exactly as planned. I surrounded myself with the right hosts, sat and spent time with dear friends, and assembled a terrific supporting cast and staff. Our team was a well-oiled machine, and the evening flowed with good pacing in an original, classic Hollywood style.

But what stuck in my mind and awoke me at 5 a.m. the following morning were the flaws ... complaints about seating arrangements, a mistyped last name, and one incorrect listing in the gorgeous program.

Walking in the hotel door that afternoon, I knew there would be things that would go awry or take their own direction. Stuff happens. Any event planner recognizes that the unexpected will arise. So, I had secured my personal version of Teflon coating, and I was ready for the challenges. I anticipated there could be elements that might escape my careful planning and meticulous double and triple checks. But, when it happened, it still threw me. Admittedly, not as much as it once would have. Yet, enough to shake me up a bit. It gets to me... the disappointment directed at me from a peer, the bitter tone of complaints when someone did not get what they expected. I do not like to let people down—to feel I have failed them in some way.

Why do we do that? Look to the flaws instead of the numerous things that go right? Why is our daily news filled with the problems instead of a celebration of achievements? Why does that "B" on the test or report card dim the shining glory of the five "As"? Why does the messy closet or dust in our house taunt us, when the rest of our home is vacuumed and clean? Why does the chipped nail or blemish overshadow the loveliness of the spirit or the rest of the individual?

Or why do we *FEEL* it does?

That morning after as I thought about the "flaws" in my evening, I vowed I would find a way to change this way of thinking. Instead of stressing, I embraced my mistakes ... confronted and apologized for them, doing whatever I could to validate the different perspective of those who did not find my event to their satisfaction. But I decided I would not accept the negativity that came with their "feedback." Instead, I made a list of everything that went right and set it down next to the list of imperfections. Then, I crumbled the list of flaws and tossed it in the trash.

That night, I had done my best. One hundred and fifty-six people, including my husband Doug, enjoyed the evening completely. I think it is fair to accept that as a success. So, three or four did not. Stuff happens.

It's easier to focus on flaws than on the good things we accomplish and achieve. As an actor, I have experienced times when a line is dropped. There is panic in the air... every performer has

On the dance floor with my husband Doug
Photo by David Reed

felt that rush of adrenalin. But, instead of focusing on the mistake, we should celebrate the recovery, how we maintained our composure and seamlessly brought the scene back on track.

In yoga, I often need to find a focal point to help me achieve balance. Invariably, I seek a knot in the wood or an imperfection in the curtain, wall, ceiling, or floor. It's just easier to find and focus on a flaw than on a smooth surface.

Huh and WOW! That was a huge "Ah-ha" discovery moment for me.

But why is that? I wonder. We are not perfect. We all know that. Why do we seek perfection and feel less successful when "stuff happens?" Mistakes, disappointments, and flaws are part of the human experience. We learn. We grow. We go on. We should celebrate that and embrace the good. Let go of the other stuff. Holding onto it just makes us dissatisfied with our own selves. What's the good in that?

My daughter Paige on pointe, a talent I never achieved

The day after the gala, after some reflection, I shook off the melancholy. I chose to celebrate the numerous things that went right and dismiss the few that were not so... ideal. If we all tried that, perhaps these little upsets that get to us and ruin an evening, experience, or relationship would fade into unimportance.

I will never get to spin on pointe shoes like my daughter does. However, I do have exceptional posture and a continued passion for ballet. No resentment or sense of failure here. I know it's hard to stay balanced and to find the good when others seek to remind you of the flaws. But I'm learning to choose where to place my focus.

So, I ask you: What will you choose as your Focal Point?

Coffee with My Cat

"A cat has absolute emotional honesty: human beings, for one reason or another, may hide their feelings, but a cat does not."
—Ernest Hemingway

t has been a long time since I have needed an alarm to wake me. That's because I have a cat. A sweet torty with sea-green eyes and an orange heart on the top of her velvety soft, furry head.

Ellie. Well, Elena Marie—a blended name inspired by Catherine Zeta-Jones' strong-willed Elena from *The Mask of Zorro* and the playful Marie from Walt Disney's *The AristoCats*. I typically call her Miss Ellie... a throwback to my devotion to the evening soap opera *Dallas*.

Ellie is my first cat. Technically—as my daughter regularly reminds me—she's *HER* cat. But Ellie is not waking my daughter up early in the morning.

Now, I did not know much about the personalities and habits of cats when we adopted Ellie. I did some research, but there were quite definitely areas of non-disclosure and things I just did not know, such as...

Torties are Talkers, and Ellie is a Chatty Cat. She is quite vocal about her wishes, needs, and desires.

At night, she sleeps at the foot of the bed, curled up by my feet. On cold nights, she prefers the warmth of my husband and sprawls out to claim space. But, at around 6:17 a.m., she emits this rumbly purr—kind of like the sound a young child makes when they want out of their crib.

It begins softly and becomes more insistent, like an alarm clock tone that grows louder and more frequent before you slam it off. But, unlike an alarm clock, Ellie does not come with a snooze button.

Sometimes I feign sleep, but Ellie is quite clever. When I finally agree to rise and shine, she sits up and stretches—languidly—as though I am the one dragging *HER* out of bed. She gazes up as if to say, "Is it that time already?" I scratch her head, and she leaps from the bed to sit near my slippers.

You would think that means she wants food, right? Nope. She just wants time with me. So, we start our routine, Ellie and me. She bounds down the stairs at my side and sits at the front door. This is her next "ask:" that I turn on "Kitty TV" and initiate screen time. It does not matter the season or temperature outside. Winter, spring, summer, and autumn, it's the same demand.

I next fill her food bowl, provide fresh water, and—only then—prepare my coffee. After she has checked out the Nature Channel, she runs to the kitchen and continues to purr, suggesting that I speed things up. I grab that important first cup of caffeine, and she meanders beside me until I sit down in my chair. Only then does she settle down. It happens every day this way, these 30 minutes with my cat.

It is a structured and extremely specific routine. Trust me, she has me well-trained. It's as if *SHE* were the Event Planner and I, her minion. Like my kids were in their younger years, Ellie is an Early Riser.

I'm not complaining... well, not most of the time. There are days I want to dive into my pillows and ignore her. There are days I do. But my early moments with Ellie are truly some of my favorite times of the day. Reflective. Quiet. Deeply spiritual. Thankful thoughts and journaling begin our day. I read my devotions as she sits with watchful eyes and her tail curled delicately. I pray. I write. I read. And we play a little, too.

During those early mornings of *Coffee-with-My-Cat*, she offers "lovey eyes," telling me how much she, too, enjoys our time. And in those moments, I know she loves me. Treasures me. Values me. And that I am important to her.

It's funny how a pet can change your life and teach you things. She truly demonstrates the unconditional meaning of love. No words are exchanged to earn it. Sure, I show her I love her in simple deeds like feeding her, cleaning her litter box, and brushing her fur. Her asks are little while what she offers is enormous. With a look, she tells me she loves me on the good days and the bad days. She reminds me that I'm enough on the exceptional days and the horrible ones. She's there for me, greeting me at the door no matter what time I arrive home, offering companionship and her own style of communication.

Lately, she's even begun joining me on the mat for yoga. She seems to have discovered something there she enjoys too. At first, I interpreted the move to the mat as a request for scratches. But I quickly found, when she moved away toward the front or back of the mat, that  she was really just there to spend time with me. She recognizes that my mat is an important place for me—and chooses to make it one for her as well. As I flow through poses, careful not to land on her since she inevitably selects a spot dead center, I can hear the rumbling sound of her purrs. Her presence speaks volumes about her choice to spend time with me... to be there *on the mat* with me.

I guess I'm like Ellie. There are special people in my life that I reach out to and try to be there for. Not at 6:17 a.m. in most cases—pretty confident that I can say they are glad about that. But there are people I call, text, write, FaceTime, email, and choose to make time for on a regular basis. These friends know who they are because I tell them regularly. I don't always get hours and hours with them. I get time here or there, based on our schedules. Life is busy. But the time we choose to share—be it moments or hours—is meaningful. It matters. It's priceless. Those moments make a difference. They make me smile, bringing lightness and joy with each connection. This time spent in a connection helps ground me or gives me energy or revs me up or even calms me down like a walk on the beach. It depends on the person, the timing, and what I need at that moment.

> *"Some people—or four-legged friends—come into our lives and quickly go. Others stay, leave footprints on our hearts, and we are never, ever the same."*
> —Flavia

I like to think I have left a few footprints on the hearts of these people who surround me and complete me, who live close by or across the miles. In our time together, hope I give—or gave—them something they needed and that it helps us remain connected when life creates distance or barriers. It's just like those 30 minutes with my cat. Ellie reaches out a paw and asks for time and love. I respond and offer Ellie what she needs. And in that quiet time, Ellie gifts me with her unconditional love.

It's simple, really. Sometimes it's locking eyes with someone special and feeling a flow of energy. Sometimes it's a hug or a smile or a light caress on my arm. Sometimes it's a hand that holds mine, a companionable drink—coffee, tea, or something stronger—or a day at the spa.

During yoga classes, it can be a gentle touch to relax a pose and remind me someone is looking out for me. Sometimes it can be a night out or shared French fries. Sometimes it's loud. Sometimes it can be found in companionable silence. Sometimes it's a circle of knitters giggling together. Sometimes it's crazy and wild. Sometimes it's laughter or tears. Sometimes it comes as a phone call, a letter received in the mail, or a text. Sometimes it's a chance to vent. Sometimes it's quiet... words unnecessary... just mutual understanding of shared feelings and experiences.

Bottom line, it's about making time for the people—and animal friends—who give our lives meaning, joy, and love. No matter if it's 30 minutes, an adventurous vacation to a far-off place, browsing a bookstore together, or a full day playing hooky, it speaks to the importance of those dear to us.

30 minutes may be all I have to give. It may be all you can give. But that time teaches us to make every moment count. Love is not finite. Taking time to spend with the people—or pets—important to us nurtures our hearts and spirits, leaving our souls caressed by the warmth of incredible joy.

Sugar & Spice

*"A daughter may outgrow your lap,
but she will never outgrow your heart."*
—Unknown

I packed away my daughter Paige's dollhouse today.

Sitting on the pink carpeting in her updated "tween"-styled room, I carefully removed tiny pieces of furniture and dusted them before placing each one carefully in the box from which I had removed them nearly nine years ago. Some of the pieces had come from my own dollhouse. Some were new to her. When it came time to pack away the tiny pink china dishes, I felt tears slipping down my face.

She once found so much joy in that dollhouse. Our discovery of it was a fluke at a garage sale. I had planned on building her one, like my parents built mine. But we "renovated" this one instead, together selecting new colors, painting it, adding hardwood flooring, kitchen tile, carpeting, and updated wallpaper, and finally decorating it with the furniture she chose. Her Lalaloopsy dolls found their home inside those walls. Many were still inside, lounging on dusty chairs and sleeping in the brass bed I had treasured once upon a time.

I remember watching her playing, moving, and speaking for the dolls—creating magical stories only she understood. I remember the many times she asked me to "play people" with her, and we sat down on the floor and imagined together.

The dollhouse, Lalaloopsies, and American Girl dolls have been left alone

*Paige and her cousin Christina
"playing people"*

for a year now. I was in denial for a while, hopeful that the days of her exploring the extraordinary, captivating widths and depths of her imagination to "play people" were not over. But, as I removed dusty furniture and dolls, I knew that time had passed. And I was seriously weeping when I carried the dollhouse to the basement and placed the boxed-up furniture on a shelf to save for Paige's children to discover.

I had been through this once before, when my son transitioned away from his once coveted Webkinz and Club Penguin membership. He packed his childhood toys away himself, though. One day they were in his room; the next they were in a box in the basement. It was a *Toy Story 3* moment—a Disney film I truly cannot watch, as it turns me into a blubbering mess every time.

> *"Letting your kids grow up is kind of like releasing a kite.*
> *You hate to see it go, but it looks so beautiful as it climbs*
> *higher and higher in the bright blue sky."*
> —Susan Gale

Paige with her Just Like Me doll, Penelope

Though the days of dolls have come to an end, I know I will enjoy new treasured times that I share with Paige. No, she will not climb on my lap and snuggle—she would crush me if she did! And she will not ask me to "play people" or invite me to a tea party with her American Girl dolls. But we will share middle school and high school dramas, Apple Music playlist, Instagram photos, boy problems, friendship struggles, drama club productions, choir concerts, and pointe ballet performances. What is ahead? I truly don't know.

But, since we have already enjoyed special times cooking and baking together, shopping for dresses for dances and clothing that fits her evolving personal style, and travelling to NYC and Disney World for girls only trips, it's bound to be exciting and wonderful—in a new way.

There will be many Sugary moments in the coming days, weeks, months, and years. Life is like that. The discomfort of Spice, as relationships twist and turn and sometimes fall away is hard to endure. Endings are difficult. Sometimes you don't see them coming. They sneak up on you, unexpected. One moment you are immersed in sweet Sugary playtime and experiencing incredible joy. Then, the story changes. You reach the end of a chapter without realizing it. Some experiences—like childhood—cannot last forever, no matter how many stars we wish upon.

As I packed away Paige's childhood treasures, a part of me was packed away too. But it's not truly an ending. It's more of a beginning of something different and a chance to look forward to what is yet to come. My daughter and I have always been close. And though her Tween to Teen years will certainly present a lot of Spice, I also recognize there will be Sugary Joy along with Special Memories created along the way, too.

And, for the record, after I cleaned out, vacuumed, and dusted her room, I settled down on the floor to change all the American Girl dolls into their fancy spring dresses, to enjoy a tea party of my own with them...

From Left to Right: Seated Penelope, Saige, Bitty Baby Mimi, and Samantha; Standing: Marie-Grace, Caroline, Felicity, & Elizabeth

Road Closed to Thru Traffic

"Nothing lasts forever. So, live it up, drink it down, laugh it off, avoid the drama, take chances and never have regrets because at one point everything you did was exactly what you wanted."
—Marilyn Monroe

The other day I was on my way to meet a friend. As I was in unfamiliar territory, I asked Google Maps to guide me to my end location. I love that. I just plug in my iPhone, push a button on the steering wheel of my Ford Escape, speak a few words and Hugh (my Siri app is an Australian male voice, so I nicknamed him Hugh, like in Hugh Jackman) directs me to my desired location.

On the way, though, I came across orange barriers with **Road Closed to Thru Traffic** in bold lettering.

Now, Hugh had not suggested another route, which he usually does if there is construction. And, since I was following his lead, and I could not see any actual issues barring my forward momentum, I proceeded to the route.

New pavement greeted me, but no other sign suggested that I should change my direction.

Another barrier soon rose before me. It was another closure sign. I was beginning to feel like I was on the old Mr. Toad's Wild Ride from Walt Disney World's Magic Kingdom. Like Mr. Toad, I decided to keep moving forward. Nothing dangerous lurked ahead. I saw no sign of construction workers or trucks. Just smooth black asphalt, newly paved and ready to support vehicles bold enough to go where no car had gone before.

I made it through the "closure" to my destination and met my friend without any complication, other than those signs. But the experience made me pause and consider.

On our journey, we come across potholes and construction, re-routing and delays, road closures, orange cones, and unexpected issues on the route we choose to take. We slow down. We accelerate. And we check the signs as we go, choosing to continue or turn to a different path. We have choices, so we weigh the pros and cons as we encounter them, doing the best we can with the information, feelings, and experience we currently have. When we see those orange posts and boldfaced signs, we have to decide if proceeding to the route is the way to go or if we should turn away and find a safer path.

I have tried both; I cannot deny it. Proceeding through the bumps, twisty dirty roads, and potholes has taught me a great deal, though there are times I would have preferred a smoother, more direct route. I have a curious, adventurous spirit that questions and explores paths others might avoid or circumvent. But this aspect of my nature has helped me grow, learn, and make amazing memories that I could have missed, had I turned from the route.

I am not sure where my Google Maps app is leading me at times. Are any of us? But I know that I have experienced great joy, much laughter, and great pleasure down the Rabbit Hole in Wonderland.

> *"Nothing lasts forever. So, live it up, drink it down,*
> *laugh it off, avoid the drama, take chances, and never*
> *regret anything, because at one point it was exactly*
> *what you wanted."*
> —Marilyn Monroe

Will I take that route again, knowing there are barriers and challenges that will meet me if I do? I do not know. Maybe. If at the end I find something worth the trip or if during the drive I make discoveries I might have missed otherwise, is it worth the risk? Maybe.

Google Maps can provide the steps to get me from A to Z. Google Maps can reroute me if I choose to turn off the street or turn away from the path. I can always request a new destination, after all. Or I can turn it off and drive without anyone influencing my path.

But these days, construction and road closures seem to be an all-year kind of thing. So, you need to pay attention, take care of yourself, and choose wisely as you drive.

I don't know what is on the route ahead for me. Does anyone, really? Google Maps and Hugh can offer direction when I'm in my car and know exactly where I need to go, but sometimes the end destination isn't quite so easily mapped. We know what we prefer. We have ideas about where we want to go and what we hope to find. So, we explore. We try different routes. We visit places that intrigue or interest us. Only then can we find what Robert Frost called "the road less traveled." Whatever that means for you and for me, I'm pretty certain that will be the path that will make all the difference for each of us.

I drive a variety of new roads these days, seeing and experiencing things I have never encountered before, facing new challenges, and new exciting opportunities. Change is part of life, re-routing happens. Knowing if I'm on the "right" path isn't always clear. Is it scary? Yes, if I'm honest.

But, if I'm honest here, I'm a passionate, curious person. I choose to live out-loud and grab life with both hands, diving in where the less bold might fear to go. That does not always make for the smoothest trip. I've been known to hit a couple of potholes now and then. Plus, unlike Google Maps, I can't predict what the next street will be or what I'll find there.

But there's one thing I do know; if what I am moving toward is important to me, well, I guess I will just have to watch the road, read the signs along the way, and decide how best to proceed as I go.

Or as dear Alice from Wonderland says, *"Begin at the beginning and go on until you come to the end, then stop."*

Keep Your Eyes on Your Own Mat

"Bloom Where You're Planted"
—Mary Engelbreit

I n yoga class the other night, we were reminded to keep our eyes focused on our own mat—that glancing around and comparing our pose to that of our neighbors did not serve us. It would not make our poses any better, and it would distract us from our own work. Chris—the yoga instructor—sagely suggested that *"comparing yourself to another person is like looking in the mirror and expecting to see someone else."*

This gentle reminder made me think about how that applies off the mat. I found myself wondering why we spend so much time rubber necking, looking at others and comparing our poses—or lives—to theirs. We seem to have a need to watch, find, or seek out what is going on at "their side of the road." What is it we hope to find? What is it we hope to gain?

I once took a yoga class where there were only two of us. Afterward, our instructor Marty mentioned how reluctant he was to lead a class with only two students. Apparently, in his previous experiences, such a session led to competition. I was stunned. It never occurred to me to compare what we were doing. The time I spend on my mat is about me. I use that time for my work. When I come to my mat, it's a time to explore my own mindfulness, strength, or lack thereof in some cases, and both spiritual and physical growth. Why would I waste that hour comparing and competing with someone else?

But, if I'm truly honest, I do it elsewhere. Many of us have areas where we are competitive. Where we want applause or recognition—or the feeling that we are somehow special or even superior. Perhaps, deep inside, we are all a little bit like Sally Field in her notable 1984 Oscar speech when she declared: *"You like me. You really like me!"* We, too, want to be liked. We want to be noticed and valued. We want to be sought after. We want to feel as though who we are and what we offer others is appreciated and important to them. We want to be desired—or at least desirable. In our heart of hearts, we long to be admired.

Take social media for example. We post something on Facebook. Why do we do that? We type something from the privacy of our own computers, phones, or tablets for the world to see. Often, if we are honest, we hope others will "Like" and comment on this post. We say something because it pops in our mind, and we want to share it. But we also do it to be noticed—to remain relevant to the outside world and our followers/friends. We place a photo, a statement, a comment, or a thought on our "Home Page," to ensure it is seen by others. And, depending upon how many friends you have, that post can be seen by a helluva lot of people.

Then, in so many cases, we sit back and watch for comments. We watch to see the likes, hearts, gifs, and emojis pop up.

Questions: *Once you've posted whatever it is you want to say, do you look back at it? How often do you check back? Do you wonder how many people liked your post? Are you curious why some people liked it or commented on it, while others did not? Do you look at posts by others and see all those likes, comments, etc., and wonder why they attracted all those "friends," while your post did not?*

That brings me back to why we post on social media in the first place. Is it simply to share a quick quip, thought, comment, observation, political/ social philosophy, stance or photograph with friends and family far and wide, or are we actively seeking to connect and communicate across the wires? Are we looking for love—or likes and thumbs ups—to support our often lonely, disconnected selves? When the responses do not come, does this increase feelings of competition and isolation?

The flowers in a garden—the roses on a large rose bush—do not look at each other and compare their blooms.

The stars in the heavens do not gaze at each other and say: "Hey, she is shining brighter than me!"

So why, in a world where a "cursor" that flashes annoyingly on a white screen, do we feel the need to seek likes and hearts on a "social" media site? And if validation is truly our goal, then perhaps we should re-evaluate the reason we log into that site to begin with.

I am guilty. I have posted a variety of blogs, photos, and thoughts and then checked back to see my stats. And there are times that I wonder why I do not have more likes. Why so- and-so does not follow me or comment or like my witty repartee. Why does so-and-so comment on another post and not mine?

It's not pretty. But I am being honest here. It's something I have done. And I don't like it or who I become when I do it. So, I've chosen to refocus my efforts to simply to bloom where I'm planted. To post and not look back. I don't look over on another person's mat to compare my yoga pose to theirs. We aren't the same people. We don't have the same flexibility or body style. Why should social media be any different? Comparing myself to another rose out there, does not make me bloom brighter, bigger, or better. No, just the opposite. It usually makes me feel inadequate, uninteresting, and needy.

> *Mary, Mary quite contrary How does your garden grow?*
> *With silver bells and cockle shells, and pretty maids*
> *all in a row.*
> —Mother Goose

Nowhere in that nursery rhyme is it suggested that the silver bells, cockle shells, and pretty maids are in competition. Nowhere does it indicate one is prettier than the others or that Mary has any desire for that to be the case.

There's freedom and joy when I simply keep my eyes on my own mat and find satisfaction in what I have offered—letting go of the rest. When I post something, I let it simply be something I want to say, share, or offer for others to take or leave. So what if only a few people discover or read it? I've said it. I've written it. I've put myself and my ideas out there. That was the point anyway.

Of course, maybe it is just me who has longings for social media approbation and acknowledgement that I'm special. Maybe it's simply my own insecurity. But I am discovering at 50+ that I really truly do not care if I am the biggest, boldest bloom in the garden. I just want to *Bloom*.

Mary Englebreit made the quote popular. But it was in France where the Bishop of Geneva, Saint Francis de Sales (1567—1622) was actually credited with the quote, *Fleuris là où tu es plantée*, which means, "Bloom where you are planted."

I seem to have figured out how to do this on my yoga mat. Maybe I can take it off the mat, too.

Turn the Page

"Sons are the anchors of a mother's life."
—Sophocles

A t 6:18 a.m. on May 12, 2020, my son turned 21.

First of all, the fact that I have a 21-year-old floors me. I wonder if my parents felt the same disbelief when I turned 21?

One minute you are holding them in your arms—a tiny, wiggly baby, incapable of doing anything on their own. Then, you are walking them to school, holding their small hand securely in your own. And then, before you know it, they want to walk to school alone. They start closing the door to their room. They stop joining you to watch TV or a movie. Then they learn to drive a car, graduate high school, and head off to college.

Thank heavens, I have a portrait in my attic that keeps me young! (*Shameless nod to Oscar Wilde.*)

Yep. Jarod has solidly stepped into his third decade. Not the most exciting year to turn 21, amidst a pandemic with bars closed and people living in a "quarantined state."

My son's senior year of high school was a very emotional time for me. And for him, as he himself understood and expressed in a final video tribute entitled "I Will Never Forget." There were so many "lasts." It was a year full of ceremonies and endings, wrapping up his first 18 years of life. Tying up his "childhood" with a neat, tidy bow and a graduation ceremony at Freedom Hill.

Summer weekends were dominated with grad parties and college planning. Then, before I knew it, we had packed up his most treasured worldly possessions and loaded them in three cars—with the help of a color-coded spreadsheet he created—to caravan to Wayne State University.

No, he did not choose a college in another state, but I promised to treat this move as if he were three hours away, guaranteeing him the freedom and independence he had shown he was ready for.

Jarod had started a new chapter all on his own in the book we had been writing together for 18 years.

He was excited—and so ready. And I was happy for him. Really, I was. But there was this part of me that felt a loss so deep that the pain was indescribable... a sense that my compass was losing its true North.

The move was easy. And he was so happy... quickly hanging posters, placing photos on his desk, and settling in. But I cried as we drove away and spent many hours just sitting in his room, missing him.

But then a strange thing happened. Calls came in. Texts to just say "Hi." There were successes or challenges in class work that he wanted to talk about. With me! Invitations for coffee or outings to the Hilberry Theatre to see a play and get dinner. To quote a song from one of his childhood favorite Disney Channel movies, it was "the Start of Something New."

The conversations changed and a new relationship began. No, he did not crawl on my lap or need me to hold his hand while he walked to class. But he still needed his Mom. He still *wanted* to share moments of his life with me. And something new and wonderful began to take shape.

Oh, I miss my sweet little boy. The "last bite thief," Barnes & Noble song-and-dance kid, and his "this is my good idea" proposals. But I treasure the opportunity to get to know the Man he is becoming as he meets the challenges of Adulting.

There are new special moments... calls where he shares what's going on, times he asks me about recipes as he prepares meals in his apartment, different outings to Barnes & Noble where we get coffee and browse non-fiction sections of the store, weekends when he comes home and says, "I just wanted to come home and be with you, Mom."

We turned the page together. And though I look back at the memories that play out in my mind like films, we now have new chapters to write as *Our Story Goes On.*

It's far too easy to look back and in so doing, miss the *Now* and all it delivers. But, coming from someone who is still featured in the script, I can honestly say the plot twists, scene changes, and character developments in the continuing adventures of Jarod Clark are a great read.

> *"Someday when the pages of my life end, I know you will be one of the most beautiful chapters."*
> —Manisha Singh Rajput

There are really no beginnings that can happen without an ending. Sometimes you have to leave behind something precious. But, if you release your hold, you might just discover that what you thought you lost, was not gone at all... just transitioning or transforming.

And there really is another chapter in the book you started all those years ago. Many of them, in fact. And this new book in the series is as good—if not better—than some of the earlier editions. I promise...

Just Breathe and turn the page.

And for heaven's sake... do not put down the book now. You are still a featured character! All relationships ebb and flow. There's so much more in the coming pages. Celebrate those moments from the earlier chapters. Relive them and smile. But keep in mind that the story goes on.

What I've learned in the past three of Jarod's college years? The diploma, graduation, and departure to college is by no means an ending of my special relationship with my son. The continuing adventures... and the fact that Jarod wants to share his Adulting with me... that's priceless!

Turn the page...

Living in Absolutes

"It was the best of times; it was the worst of times..."
—Charles Dickens

So begins the classic novel written by Charles Dickens in 1859. It was a book set during the Reign of Terror, leading up to and including the French Revolution. It dealt with human struggle. It dealt with social injustice and great darkness. It dealt with fear and loss, death and survival, darkness and light. It is widely considered Dickens' greatest work and is one of the best-selling classic novels of all time.

Along comes 2020. It is the best of times... it is the worst of times. It is the year we were quarantined in our homes. It is the year international travel stopped and Walt Disney World shut down. It is the year businesses sent workers away from their offices to work remotely. It is the year we found ourselves separated from loved ones and people we care about. It is the year the phrase "social distancing" was coined. It is the year sporting teams, theatres, and movie houses locked their doors and cancelled events, games, and performances. It is the year fitness studios began hosting virtual exercise classes. It is the year we downloaded Zoom onto our electronic devices—the year "Zoom" became more than a zany 1970's kids show on PBS. It is the year awareness and outrage about social injustice at long last prompted action. It is the year our youth and college students began virtual learning, attending school and college classes on-line at home.

It is the year we began wearing masks.

2020—from all social media postings and professional commentary—is the Worst of Times. Social distancing and masks are the new normal. As I write this, many aspects of our society are still shut down. Sporting events continue, but without fans in the stands. While we can visit spas and eat in restaurants, seating is limited, and people must wear masks and have their temperatures taken to enter. Protests and riots rage across the country, bringing to the surface years of anger and resentment—years of injustice due to the color of a person's skin. People rise up... but we struggle to find a cohesive plan and voice to finally make that critical change.

I am one of them.

Like those moments in history considered the "worst" of times, that so many of us remember vividly—such as the Kennedy assassination and the World Trade Center attack—we all can recall where we were on March 12, 2020, when the NBA cancelled its season. We can recall that last dinner out before restaurants closed, the last friend we hugged as we said our goodbyes after a night of laughter and conversation, or our last workout inside the walls of a fitness studio. We can all recall the stay-at-home orders and the moment when six feet of separation became our reality.

Yet... in *A Tale of Two Cities*, Dickens combined the sentiments. He said it was the Best of Times *and* the Worst of Times. And he began with "the Best" not "the Worst," in his famous opening sentence. That structure gives me hope and challenges me to look at these times in a different light.

During this Worst of Times, there are still some "Best of" moments. A shadow cannot form without light behind it. During a Reign of Terror like we are experiencing right now, we need to bring those Best of moments into to the forefront of our thinking.

The community theatre I perform with shut down. But I was in a fabulous show only a few months before the doors were closed. I appreciated the experience and people then. I'm grateful I had that experience and creative opportunity even more now.

My yoga studio locked its doors, but the virtual classes they now offer have introduced me to new teachers I would never have met, given me the chance to take more classes than ever before, and even allowed me attend Rooftop Yoga classes over the summer, which are held on the top of a local parking structure. Watching the sunset doing yoga is mind-blowing. These days, my body is in better shape than ever before. And mentally, with the additional meditation time, I'm more focused and grounded than I have been in a very long time. Plus, I get to do virtual yoga with my cat!

A friend who lives too far away for regular outings suggested a 5:01 p.m. FaceTime Happy Hour once a week. We have been meeting weekly for either Happy Hour or Coffee Hour since March. Our friendship has never been stronger.

During the height of the pandemic, my son turned 21. Longtime friends— friends who have known him since the night he was born—took time to drive by, drop a six-pack of beer or adult beverage on the sidewalk, and wish him well. No bar night... no party... no matter. The kindness and thoughtfulness of their efforts spoke volumes. It created a connection that this time of separation cannot destroy.

That theatre I mentioned hosts an annual gala. Since it could not happen live, I had a chance to help create a "virtual" experience for the members. And— bonus—it created an opportunity for a creative challenge, a filming/acting project that a friend and I jumped on! It then wrapped up with a nice dinner for six. We found a way to socialize, connect, and celebrate anyway—in a less extravagant, more genuine way.

Two of my girlfriends and I took a trip up to the Leelanau, Michigan area for a wine-tasting, get-out-of-town long weekend. I would never have been able to do something like this if I were working full-time. But with everything happening in our world, we made a choice to slow down one weekend and take some time away, together, time to laugh, drink wine, and dedicate a few days to enjoy some selected, simple moments. It was the Best of Times.

With friends Cheryl and Mandy at Big Little Wines in Michigan's Leelanau Peninsula

"Wine and friends are a great blend."
—Ernest Hemingway

I am not saying that a global pandemic is a good thing. Many people have died. People I personally knew are now a "statistic." People are suffering and struggling. Lost jobs and lost income—lost opportunities and an altered state—have resulted in depression and increased anxiety for many. These are difficult times. That is our truth right now.

But if you look at your own life, perhaps you too can find some light in the tunnel—some "Best of Times" in the midst of all this "Worst."

We have learned to better appreciate people we *CAN* finally see and to make the most of the time we spend time with them. We have learned to appreciate slower days with puzzles, Netflix, and walks while the movie theatres and gyms are closed. We have found ways to be together, safely. We have made time for the people and the activities that matter most. And we have learned—well, I have learned—that losing a job has the potential to propel me to action I might not have taken, opening doors I might not have tried. Oh, those doors might be jammed right now, but I will find the key. I believe the next right thing *IS* out there.

If we truly view this as the Worst of Times, we do ourselves a disservice if we fail to look deeper and recognize the Bests in it too. The Bests we might have missed, had we been rushing along at our pre-March 12 pace. After all, if you read the WHOLE first paragraph of Mr. Dickens book, there is a perspective there that transcends the 18th Century... a perspective that we can bring into 2020 and our struggling world.

There is never just The Worst. If we insist on living in absolutes, what goes down, must come up. It is like we are riding a teeter-totter. We balance for a time and then—even if our side goes down—we will eventually come back up.

Check out *A Tale of Two Cities.*

> *"It was the best of times, it was the worst of times, it was the age of wisdom, it was the age of foolishness, it was the epoch of belief, it was the epoch of incredulity, it was the season of Light, it was the season of Darkness, it was the spring of hope, it was the winter of despair, we had everything before us, we had nothing before us, we were all going direct to Heaven, we were all going direct the other way—in short, the period was so far like the present period, that some of its noisiest authorities insisted on its being received, for good or for evil, in the superlative degree of comparison only."*

A TALE OF TWO CITIES —Charles Dickens

Cinnamon Toast, J.J. Newberry, and A Sycamore Tree

"Never lose the ability to see through the eyes of a child."
—Matthew T. Troyer

When I was a little girl, I traveled to visit my grandparents regularly. I was lucky to have two sets of grandparents who lived relatively close together. My mom's parents lived in a city with museums and a set of cousins to play with. My dad's parents resided in a small town about an hour South of there.

I loved both places and my experiences there. Yet, I find myself thinking so often about that small town. It is odd, really, because the person I am today revels in her proximity to city life. But, if I'm honest, there was something about Martinsville, Indiana that fascinated me—something that left a mark.

I loved my grandparents' house. It had character. The very first thing I did when I visited was to pull out the magic drawer where Grandmother kept all the kid books—titles I only glimpsed during my time there. And then I had to run to the kitchen to check, first: the candy drawer and second: the pies sitting on the counter. No matter what else she baked before we arrived, Grandmother always made two small personal pies: chocolate crème for my brother and coconut crème for me. She was an exceptional cook.

Then there was the cinnamon toast that Grandmother used to make us for breakfast. She would cut it into bite size pieces or strips and serve it on a tray as we watched our Saturday morning cartoons. I think my brother and I ate a loaf between us every morning we were there.

I treasured the adventures that took place when I visited Martinsville. It had this magical "dime store," located at the corner of Hemphill and Jefferson, called J.J. Newberry. When we visited, my brother Jeff and I couldn't wait to climb into Granddaddy's car and drive to a downtown that actually featured a

"square," complete with a courthouse in the center. J.J. Newberry had dark, dusty wood floors with aisles full of priceless treasures waiting to be discovered. Jeff and I would take our time examining every possibility before each selecting the one special present that our Grandparents would purchase for us. I remember some of my treasures: a mini baby doll who cried real tears, silly putty, quiz magazines that revealed hidden pictures when colored with special pens, toy figures on which you pressed the bottom button and they collapsed like broken marionettes.

Even now J.J. Newberry glistens magically in my mind.

There was also this restaurant and candy store called the Candy Kitchen. Grandmother would take me there for milkshakes and sweet treats. You know the kind of place—one that made the chocolate chip milkshakes with honest-to-goodness real mini chocolate chips. We would sit in a chipped, green-painted booth that was better than anything the Plaza Hotel could offer, waiting for a teenage waitress to "pull" a real cherry soda from the fountain. Then, before we would leave, we shopped for a bag of penny candy, licorice bites for me, orange slices for my brother, and cinnamon pieces for my dad.

My grandparents, Iva and Willard Carmichael, on their wedding day

One of my favorite places to go during my stays at 540 E. Harrison Street was Jimmy Nash Park. It was a delightful place where kids could explore and play on metal play structures—years before plastic took over. There was a rocket ship with multi-levels and slides, monkey bars, and even a wooden merry-go-round. Next to this park was an enormous hill. The kind you just had to roll down. And we did!

I remember outings in Granddaddy's car to Turkey Run Station Park, about an hour South of Martinsville. Grandmother would make a fried chicken picnic lunch. We would sing songs all the way there. Granddaddy had a powerful voice, and he loved to sing. Once we arrived, Granddaddy would take us hiking while Grandmother took care of the picnic preparations. Then we would sit together and laugh and talk and just spend time. No matter what we were doing, we were connected and together. I don't know if I noticed that then. But as I ride along now with my kids sorting through iPhone apps, watching DVDs wearing noise-cancelling headphones, and enraptured by electronic entertainment, I recognize the power of those childhood moments. There were large family dinners after church with Granddaddy's sisters our cousins all gathered for a meal at Poe's Cafeteria—I always ate fried chicken, green beans, and pie! Days rolled along with an easy, unhurried pace.

One other thing I recall. There was this enormous sycamore tree. It had been there long before the land it sat on became a town. I visited it every time I traveled there. Granddaddy and I would go for lots of walks, and we would always stop by to visit this tree. Did you know that sycamore trees, as they age, lose all their bark? Well, this tree had absolutely no bark. It was ancient. And it absolutely fascinated me.

My grandparents on their Golden Anniversary

It has been an exceedingly long time since I have been to Martinsville. My grandparents have both passed away. The goodbyes were difficult, but Grandmother's passing closed a chapter in a book that had reached its final pages.

After her funeral, my brother, cousin, dad, mom, husband, sister- in-law, aunt, and I went to the park... the one with the rocket ship. My brother and I climbed inside that rocket. At 29, it was as wonderful as at age 9. The treasured memories came alive. The absolute best part of that awful day was

when we all rolled down that big hill, laughing out loud, and remembering my Grandparents and the times they brought us to the park to play. And then, a few of us walked to visit the sycamore tree. I gazed at it, in awe after all those years. It had been struck by lightning, but was still standing as proud, strong, and magnificent as it had always been. But I knew I was saying Goodbye to it that day.

J.J. Newberry closed its doors ages ago. The Candy Kitchen went out of business during an economic downturn, though the candy shoppe is still around and remains famous for its candy canes. My brother Jeff and his wife Marcy make it a point to include a Candy Kitchen candy cane in our Christmas stockings each year.

The Park replaced all the "dangerous" metal equipment with plastic playscapes. And the sycamore tree—*My Sycamore Tree*—was removed. I guess people thought it might fall in its post-lightning struck state. Nothing remains. Even the new owners of the property located at Sycamore and Pike Street, where the tree once stood, know nothing of its long-time presence there.

But that tree was incredibly strong; I know it would have survived. It was simple. Pure. Like my childhood days in Martinsville. Just spending time. Singing songs. Taking walks. Enjoying popcorn prepared with care on the stove. Savoring meals—like homemade beef and noodles—made lovingly from scratch and served around the same table on which we played card games late into the evenings. We did not spend long hours in front of the TV. We read books sitting outside in the clover, helped Granddaddy in his garden, or just played outside. The music came from the radio or record player. A grandfather clock told us the time, and one bathroom that we all shared. It was truly the simple joy found in being together that resonates strongest with me to this very day. It was never the big moments that made my time in Martinsville so special. It was the little things we did together that stand out in my mind, even decades after they occurred.

I still hear Granddaddy's voice leading the singing when I recall those Martinsville adventures.

I wonder what my kids will remember when they think about special moments growing up. Is there still wonder today in the midst of high-tech, TVs with hundreds of channels, iPhones, and Nintendo? The Game Days of Sunday afternoons have been replaced with Wii tournaments and only the occasional board game marathon. We don't sing when we take long drives. Instead, my kids watch DVDs or YouTube videos. But we do have movie afternoons, and the kids and I bake and frost cookies together. We've enjoyed many nice long hikes on a number of family vacations.

> *"It is the sweet simple things in life which*
> *are the real ones after all."*
> —Laura Ingalls Wilder

We can still make special moments today. They are just... different. If we devote time to enjoy being with the people we love and focus on what is important, we discover simple, uncomplicated pleasure. I think about what I remember from childhood and bring that into my actions today. I share my passions with my kids—and they share theirs with me. Oh, I'm not sure everyone is as sentimental as I am... and I don't know if my Grandparents truly realized the long-term joys they provided with their simple outings and sharing. I like to think they knew though.

That giant sycamore may not stand in Martinsville anymore, but it survives strongly in my mind. It is a symbol of strength and perseverance, of laughter and family outings, of game nights and singing on long car trips, and drawers with books, cinnamon toast and personal coconut cream pies.

It is a symbol of how powerful the simplest moment truly is.

How Many Reps Left?

"It took me a long time to realize, we are not
meant to be perfect; we're meant to be whole."
—Jane Fonda

D o you exercise? It has been a part of my life for so long, I don't know how *NOT* to exercise. I am one of those sick people who misses it when I don't get that workout in. Exercise connects my mind, spirit, and body like nothing else. Exercise gives me clarity.

I enjoy exercise. It's not a tagline or something I say and do not do. I have honestly been following some sort of work out regime since the Jane Fonda aerobics routine came out, circa... well a while ago.

If I think back on it, my workout addiction began when my aunt gave me a couple "aerobics" outfits and legwarmers. (Yes, I was a Flashdance girl!) I began taking aerobics while my father played racquetball. This continued throughout high school and into college, where I taught aerobics in one of Albion College's gathering spaces. And my "habit" was supersized as I neared 29, when a friend told me how things started shifting on her body. Well, damned if I was going to "shift." So, I set out to find a way to keep all aspects of me in the places I wanted them.

Vanity, thy name is Jenni.

I had a goal to stay in shape. I liked how I looked and felt after working out. That was enough incentive for me as I began *The Firm* workouts with weights. The dopamine rush I feel after a yoga practice, a swim, a Barre3 routine, or even a brisk walk tells me that I am doing something good for my mind and body.

But there is another aspect that I believe we can all relate to, a common denominator to appreciate when it comes to exercise. This morning, in the midst of my routine, I was doing a certain number of repetitions. That is how you tone muscle and get rid of fat, right? Repetition of a specific movement is how you make the body better. Repeat a specific behavior and get the results you want. That's the formula.

So, there I am in full workout mode, feeling the burn. No matter the rush you receive by working out, there is a defining moment you look forward to: The End! The question in your mind at various moments during an exercise regime becomes: *How many more reps? How much longer? When will my suffering—I mean, this challenge—end? 30 reps? 2 miles? 20 more minutes? How long do I have to hold this pose? How long must I balance on one leg? How long until I can move to child's pose and just breathe?*

Exercise time parallels life. There are movements—and moments—where everything is smooth. You feel good and you are enjoying that "pose." Or you are in rhythm on a run. Whatever it is... it is flowing smoothly. You are lost in the breath or the stride.

But, as the repetitions continue and the tension in your muscles grows, you begin to long for an end. A resolution. A pay-off. You anticipate that ultimate finale when you can stop and celebrate completion and at long last enjoy the promised results.

In yoga, there are poses you enjoy and poses you struggle with. For me, I LOVE Triangle pose or any twisting pose. But send me to Chair Pose or Curtsy Squat and my muscles start to shake like crazy. Ask me to hold too long in Majorette, Boat Pose or King Dancer, and I am a quaking mess.

I know when I hold those poses, or when I do those numerous repetitions, that I don't have to hold on or repeat forever. There is always an end in sight. I have to admit, though, that I appreciate the instructor giving me a countdown. Even if I know I have 30 more reps or a 10 second hold, I also know there is an end in sight. I am assured that things will get better... that I will move differently... that I won't shake forever. I know there is a moment in the not-so-distant future when the "struggle" will end. And I know, ultimately, that it will be worth all the effort.

My family does a lot of hiking. We traveled to both North Carolina and, more recently, the Smokey Mountains. While on vacation there, the paths we selected and explored were often steep, multiple mile hikes. In some cases, we didn't know long it would take to reach the top or how convoluted the climb might become along the way. There was even one hike where we found ourselves lost!

I recall a hike my husband and I took this past summer to see a waterfall. Along the way, we passed a deer grazing on the path, but no other people. We climbed across trees that formed "bridges," our footfalls the only sound.

Then, we began to feel raindrops and hear thunder in the distance, but we kept climbing. The path was narrow, and dirt, rock, and root covered. Mile markers came and went, but we didn't have a trail- map to advise us how much longer we would be climbing. And, we didn't know exactly what we might discover when we finally reached the top. Would it be worth all the effort? But we kept moving forward. And the payoff at the end—the glorious waterfall in that solitary area of the Smokey Mountains—was absolutely worth the climb!

In whatever exercise program you choose, you KNOW that the pose, the move, or the lap will eventually change and end. But when you are in the midst of it, you don't have an actual concept of how long that might take. You may mentally recognize that you will move into something different, perhaps easier, or more personally satisfying. However, you have to choose to buckle down and just keep going to reach the wrap up. Runners know that the route has a cool-down point where they slow down and stop. Swimmers understand the distance or number of laps required. If you take a yoga or Barre3 class, lift weights, or do aerobics, you recognize the length of the workout. And you cherish the knowledge that no matter how long it takes, you grow stronger in the midst of it all.

> *"Not knowing when the dawn will*
> *come, I open every door."*
> —Emily Dickinson

When life gets uncertain and dark clouds come your way, you don't know how long it will last. When rejection and disappointment cast shadows on your path and leave you feeling lonely and alone, you don't know if anyone or anything will come along to brighten the broken cobblestones before you. When friends disappear, when you lose a job, or sickness hits you or a loved one, you don't know when the prognosis will improve.

All you have is the hope that, eventually, you will change the pose. That eventually an instructor—or a guiding friend or force—will help you discover hidden strength to cling to in those moments when your body is shaking and requesting help from someplace deeper inside. You just have to trust yourself and know that you can and *will* find it.

You can ask the universe, "How many reps are left?" but don't expect an answer. Just know it will be enough to get you to where—or how—you need to be. It's all part of the process of self-surrender, a significant behavior modification that eventually leads to transformation of the personality, of the spirit, of the mind, of the body, and of the heart.

"How many reps left?" I ask, panting and sweating and struggling.

"When does it get easier?" I wonder, as I shake during that difficult pose.

"When will I catch a break and win the day?" I wonder, after the audition or the interview or the meeting.

"When will I understand?" I wonder, after that phone call.

The universe is silent. All I can do is keep moving and trust the process. In life, we don't know how many repetitions remain. But we do know that eventually, and just like in yoga—in its time—the pose will change.

Whooo...are...you?

"Who are you?" said the Caterpillar.

This was not an encouraging opening for a conversation.
Alice replied, rather shyly, "I—I hardly know, Sir, just at present—
at least I know who I was when I got up this morning, but I
think I must have been changed several times since then.
—Lewis Carroll's Alice's Adventures in Wonderland

Alice is my favorite character in literature. I admire her inquisitive nature, her determination, and her willingness to leap into the Rabbit Hole fearlessly. I love her desire to explore and accept what happens to her. I love that she is curious. I have read both her stories repeatedly.

In Lewis Carroll's nonsensical world, there resides a caterpillar. He is now, thanks to the cleverness of Tim Burton, known as Absalom. And his voice echoes in my head—sounding, not surprisingly, very much like Alan Rickman. His key question applies not only in a whimsical land to Alice, but to each of us. No matter whether we are 3" tall and standing beside a mushroom or 5'6" tall walking down the street, we must consider a very personal and sincere question, as only we can answer it genuinely:

Whooo... are... you?

Intriguing and not easily answered, is it?

Hamlet examined this very question in one of his many contemplative monologues, lamenting: *"What a piece of work is a man! How noble in reason, how infinite in faculty! In form and moving, how express and admirable! In action how like an angel, in apprehension how like a god! The beauty of the world. The paragon of animals. And yet, to me, what is this quintessence of dust?"*

Bringing us back to The Caterpillar. *"Whooo... are... you?"* he asks in breathy tones. The answer, even for Alice, was more complicated than she first realized. And so it is with each of us.

Whooo... are... you?

Perhaps you are many things, making the answer elusive. Mother or Father, Wife or Husband, Significant Other, Lover, Actor, Athlete, Singer, Dancer, Writer, Director, Explorer, Poet, Doctor, Lawyer, Indian Chief?

Perhaps you have a job or career, in the home or outside its four walls. Perhaps you have a hobby or a passion. Perhaps you like to garden or dance. Perhaps you teach or guide others at a school or other facility. Perhaps you are an animal lover or retired after many years in the work force.

Your beliefs affect who you are. Your values do, too, along with your goals and your hopes. Your deepest longings and desires. Your habits and addictions. The music you listen to and the books you select, all these things shape who you are... all these things add depth and pieces to the puzzle that is you.

There are so many possibilities and responses, leaving the Caterpillar's question floating in the air.

> *Are we who we want to be?*
>
> *Are we who others need us to be?*
>
> *Or... are we both? And did we set aside who we are—our own "muchness"— for the ease and comfort of others... or the ease and comfort of ourselves?*

In the 1970's, Sally Field played Sybil, a woman with multiple personality disorder. She had so many personalities even her therapist, played by JoAnne Woodward, did not truly know them all.

On the popular HBO series *Game of Thrones*, we met a man with many faces... Jaqen H'ghar. He can be all things or no one. His true face and motives are as unclear as why our favorite characters seem to die off all too quickly.

In these "dramas," we catch glimpses of a deeper truth... the complexity of human nature. We are each of us, a Sybil, with many characters lurking inside and awaiting a chance to come into the light. Based on the situation in which we find ourselves, we become the personality and character that fits the occasion.

We are each a Jaqen H'ghar, sometimes showing our true face and other times hiding our authentic selves in favor of donning the image our immediate situation requires—the one we select that depicts the image expected. Sometimes we hide our true face, fearing rejection or misunderstanding. Perhaps it becomes habit to show only the persona that fits the expectations of others or that meets the needs of our current situation, hiding away those darker or more rebellious elements of our personality, choosing to share them only selectively. Sometimes we choose to play the role that goes with the flow and causes the least amount of discord in our lives.

Whooo... are... you?

That is our greatest secret, isn't it? And some people keep that answer close to the vest, showing only the merest hint of its complexity to others. Some of us try to control it, manage it. No matter what words are uttered from our lips or what actions we take, only we know what is natural, what comes from the heart, what is part of our performance, and what is authentic.

Then, no matter what or who we think we are, and what we think is right or best for us, if we are open to it, we can be surprised and discover unexpected elements inside us. At any time in our lives, we can still be shaped and grow based on the words, ideas, and invitations of others...

For example, several years ago, I auditioned for a beautiful play called *Enchanted April.* I prepared and met with a friend prior to the audition to read through the script. We were auditioning for different roles and hoping to have the chance to perform together. Then, when the auditions began, the director flipped us... seeing us in the opposite roles. After months of preparing for one part, suddenly we looked at the script and roles differently. We were surprised, yet the challenge of finding ourselves in this new light helped us discover something new—something exciting and unexpected. Something enchanting in and of itself.

Providence? All I realized in that moment is that when you open yourself, you grant yourself permission to live fully and embrace unexpected opportunities.

Of our true selves, only we know. And every now and then, someone touches our lives to shed light on aspects of us even we did not recognize were hidden inside. The trick, I have discovered, is to be open to the surprises that greet us each day. We need to make the most of those moments and embrace life. We can choose to be unafraid and discover our own "muchness" by leaping down a Rabbit Hole or into the Looking Glass, coming face to face with a White Rabbit and Blue Caterpillar.

In the immortal words of *The X-Files*, "The Truth Is Out There." You can hide your Light (or your Dark), or you can leap into the Rabbit Hole, embrace each moment and person that touches your life with two hands, and continue the adventure...

What's Next?

"Life is about not knowing, having to change, taking the moment, and making the best of it without knowing what's going to happen next. Delicious ambiguity."
—Gilda Radner

Throughout our lives, we ask "What's Next?" We are impatient creatures. We want a glimpse around the corner into our future. We want to know if Something Is Coming and what that Something might be!

What's next dangles before us like a carrot—luring us on with the potential to be better, more exciting, or simply a release from the boredom or stress of this current moment. But as we look around the corner, we neglect the opportunity to make the most of and learn from what is currently before us—be it good or bad, challenging, or smooth sailing.

This happens more often when situations are challenging. We want to get past the difficult or uncomfortable moments into the fun and happy... into the easy.

In a recent yoga class, my instructor Suzanne brought this up when we moved into our first Chair pose. Well, I had bruised my tailbone the previous day when I fell ice skating, so I was not at all sure how my body would react. Once settled in, I felt a strong desire to get to the next pose. And though I could blame my initial concern on my injury, my longing to move had nothing to do with a bruised tailbone and everything to do with the difficulty of the pose. It was hard. My muscles were shaking. I wanted desperately to move on to something else.

Of course, Suzanne knew that. Heck, no one is ever "comfortable" in Chair pose. But she encouraged us to stay there... to embrace the challenge of that particular moment while maintaining our calm. She encouraged us to turn our attention to the breath and let that shifted focus help us through whatever discomfort we might be experiencing, to discover strength in the shaking and in our selves.

So, when Suzanne brought up this idea in yoga, it resonated deeply. This is a philosophy that extends into daily life. When faced with difficult times, struggles, or dissatisfaction with wherever we are and whatever perceived difficulties we are experiencing, our instinct urges us to get out of that moment. We want out of the pain, difficulty, or sadness. We want excitement or a new challenge. We feel uncomfortable, so we want the next pose or the next project, job, opportunity, relationship, etc.

We just want what is next.

And what do we do with instinctual urge? Sadly, it is not always good.

When the "now" struggle begins to take its toll, we tend to seek a quick fix. Instead of breathing and staying calm, we self-medicate with pills and alcohol in an effort to cope with anxiety, stress, or emotional pain. We bolt away from relationships and isolate. We escape into television programs to lose ourselves. We distract ourselves with something instead of dealing with the issue. We struggle with regrets and practice self-judgment. We shop and buy stuff on-line to make us "happy." We over-eat. We run away and lack conviction to confront and deal with our inner dialogue and struggles. We look ahead instead of settling into where we are and allowing whatever transformation has begun to complete the process.

We want out of the discomfort and whatever isn't *"this."* What is next is inevitably better than what we are dealing with now.

Or we think it will be.

In Slow Flow yoga, there are many common poses. However, the order differs with every class and every instructor. When we begin, I don't know what is next. I don't know what's coming or what to expect. So, I let go, which isn't something I do lightly. And it feels so good and affirming when I make it through challenging poses and moments on my mat. When I release control and accept that what comes next will be what it is—whether it is something I like, something I don't like, or something that I've never done before.

I shake. I even fall sometimes. But I keep breathing. It's just yoga. If I fall over or fall down, I can simply shake it off and get back on my feet. That's really all that matters, because when I can do that on the mat, I can learn to keep my calm—even when I don't know what's coming my way in the "real world."

> *"So I'll walk through this night, stumbling blindly toward the light. And do the next right thing."*
> —Anna, Walt Disney's Frozen 2

I am a planner. I like control. It's soothing to know what's next. Organizing and lists are my daily companions. But when I look back over my life so far, what I expected and what happened, well, they were not necessarily what I had on the list. I wake up in the middle of the night—that's not on my list, but I have to deal with it. I have issues with a friend or at work—also not on the list, but I can choose how to handle it. I've yet to experience an event I've planned that doesn't have some kerfuffle. But I'm not going to shut down. I'm going to find a way thru.

And that's what makes me stronger.

The good, the bad, the super awful, the amazing, and the ugly have made me the woman I am today. I am honestly not sure I would have wanted to know all the "stuff" I would need to deal with in advance. It might have impeded my choices and my adventure.

What's Next?

I don't know. Life has a way of throwing curve balls and putting a wrench into the most idyllic of plans.

When it happens that way, it *IS* still a Grand Adventure. Despite bumps in the ice that cause you to take a tumble or two, the skating is amazing. I've enjoyed gliding across the ice with only the sounds of my skates cutting through. It's an incredible experience. Want to know one thing I've discovered? Sometimes what you find when you *fall* on the ice is strength to get back up and keep skating. But, if you knew you were going to get hurt—if you knew you were going to fall, bruise your tailbone, and get ice chips all over yourself, might you have avoided the rink altogether? And thus, might you have missed out on something utterly amazing?

What's Next?

On the mountains and in the ravines of life, there is always change. You never stay in the same place. In yoga, Chair Pose is temporary—as are the difficulties, challenges, and even joyful moments we experience every single day.

My advice is to "Just keep breathing and stay present." You just may discover a depth of strength you didn't realize you had—and perhaps even develop some gratitude for the challenges thrown in your path.

The Choices We Make

"If the chaos is overwhelming, I start making lists.
To write it down puts it in perspective."
—Renee Lawless

I have dust on my ceiling fan.

The other night, I climbed in bed after a long day, book in hand, ready to settle in and transport myself to another place and enjoy someone else's story. After fluffing the pillows, my eyes traveled up to my high arched ceiling, to the white fan. What did I see? Dust—all the way to the edges, coating the fan blades.

Now, this is not the norm for my space. I am a Type A Neat-Freak. I clean every single Saturday without conscious thought. I like order in my home. I actually like to clean and have a routine. I love those vacuum marks in the carpet—you know what I'm talking about. Well, they make me really happy. Dust free surfaces, and mirrors without fingerprints or "schmutz" make me smile. But the ceiling fan is way up high. I need a special ladder to reach it. Cleaning that fan requires a specific decision to bring the ladder from the garage all the way upstairs, climb up, and reach for those blades.

What did I do? I looked away and returned my complete and total focus to my book.

For a long-time, I was a stay-at-home mom. In the early years of my kids' lives, I not only changed diapers, read books, played games on all fours, made up songs, and got them to and from playdates, but I also made baby food from scratch and took care of all the normal house stuff too... laundry, washing floors, meal-planning, cleaning, cooking, etc.

My husband did his share, of course. Still does! I couldn't have made it through those early years—or the later parenting years—without his support. He's an exceptional cook, grilling artist on the Big Green Egg, and the guy during holidays and everyday meals who jumps in to help with the preparation as well as wash the dishes. (He's very well aware that I'm not a fan of scrubbing dishes or dirty pans!) Doug has no issues helping me clean the house. He not only humors my neat-nick tendencies, but also accepts them with compassion.

However, in those earliest years of parenthood, I was the one at home all day long with the children. That meant that I not only saw the dust-bunnies and messes, but I felt the compulsive *NEED* to take care of them as part of my stay-at-home gig. As Doug's dad told him many years ago: "If you're going to do a job half-assed, don't do it at all." And there was no way I was going to do my stay-at-home mom job half-assed!

During their formative years, I actually worked from home too. *(Love that statement... like I was not "working" at home already.)* I had numerous clients and handled marketing, events, and communications projects along with the kids/home activities. When my son was first born, I was in the midst of planning a huge event to take place at Chicago's Palmer House Hilton Hotel. I spent many days with him propped on my leg while I typed, planned, and organized. I managed the "event, communications, and marketing work" while he napped, too. And then, when my daughter came along, I started a job with Shakespeare Royal Oak—a company that produces the works of Shakespeare in a local park—running events and handling miscellaneous other elements associated with running a professional theatre organization. It was part of what I did each day. I just happened to do it with two kids in tow.

I remember a day at the park, waiting for the port-a-johns to be delivered. My kids were playing on the playscape while I dealt with the guy setting them up. I was multi-tasking and loving every minute. It's honestly amazing what a person can handle. I like to work and be busy. I don't sit and do nothing well. I typically have a knitting project in hand as I watch TV. It's rare that I just stop. And if I do, I fall asleep.

But back to this ceiling fan. In that moment, I made a choice. I made a choice that reading my book was the priority. And when I "worked" at home while my kids were younger, I made other choices.

I chose to take them to the bookstore for a reading session and cookies, instead of washing the floor. I chose to snuggle up and play "people" with Paige instead of folding laundry. I chose to order pizza for dinner so we could spend just a little more time coloring. I chose to play two hours of *Wadget* with Jarod instead of doing chores while my infant daughter napped. I chose to rake the leaves and allow them to mess them up by jumping in them—even though it created more work for me—instead of

sweeping them to the curve and sending the kids inside. I chose to plant the flowers with their help, even when it took twice as long.

> *"Remember, the choices we make today,*
> *shape the people we become tomorrow."*
> —Victoria Osteen

I make other choices too. I choose to audition and perform in a play, knowing it will eat up time and take lots of energy and that my house will probably not be as clean for a little while since I also *still* choose to make time first for my family and friends.

I choose to host an annual birthday party for Paige and her friends instead of going somewhere else, even though it involves lots of creativity and planning, and the house will need to be cleaned and then will be a mess and need to be cleaned again. I do this even though the screaming and giggling girls will drive me crazy for few hours. Even though I have to gather all the favors instead of paying someone else to do it.

When they were younger, I didn't sleep in. I chose to get up early on Saturday mornings, first taking Jarod to swimming, then Paige to swimming, then driving Jarod to a Boy Scout event, then going to yoga, then driving home to clean the

house and host some friends for dinner and a game night. My husband and I alternated the Saturday driving experience—and dinner prep—because it offered us precious time with the kids to explore what was important to each of them and be part of that too!

I choose to get up early to work-out, instead of sleeping in. I choose to get my nails done, take my kids out to their favorite restaurant for dinner, play a Wii tournament and then, once they are in bed, settle in on a Friday night for a *Scandal* marathon 'til midnight.

I choose to volunteer and plan events though it takes lots of time, lists, and meetings. I choose to go to the bar with my friends and laugh and talk when I know I have to get up early the next day and go to work.

I choose to take the time to drive down to Indianapolis to celebrate my mom's birthday, enjoying an afternoon with her and my sister-in-law, Marcy, at *Cake Bake* for lunch, cocktails, and the most incredible sparkly cake I have ever eaten. I choose to make the time to just be with them, browsing used bookstores, strolling around downtown Carmel, and eventually settling together around the firepit to listen to my mom share her childhood memories. I choose to make time to travel there with Doug, Jarod, and Paige to enjoy time with my parents, my brother and his wife, and my nieces. I choose to put family ahead of most things.

I choose to make time for the people I care for. I choose to spend my energy on the aspects of life that I enjoy—people and projects that feed my spirit, body, and mind. I thrive as a result of these choices.

My parents, Ellen and Jim Carmichael, celebrating her 82nd birthday

And I also choose, when the demands of life wear me down, to take time to restore. I retreat to a quiet place for solitude and self-care. It's not an indulgence. It's a necessity, enabling me to reboot and recharge. I find peace on my yoga mat or sitting with a book in my library or back yard. I take my paddle board to the water. I binge the

Hallmark channel. I schedule a *Me Day* at my happy place—Beach House Day Spa. Or I just turn off my devices and create my own home spa bliss with items my niece Chris creates for me. Her lavender bath salts and stress-away lotions soothe my busy mind and weary body.

What do you choose? What are your priorities? Do these choices feed your spirit or challenge your mind? Strengthen your body or soul? Do they give you satisfaction or pleasure? Do they make you happy? What do they say about the person you are—or the person who want to be?

I guess that's what it all comes down to. What I choose reflects the person I am. What I choose reflects what I deem to be most important. I am happy with my choices.

So, dust on that ceiling fan, you will just have to wait. I have other priorities today.

My Own Worst Enemy

"Being left alone, with my mind,
is actually quite dangerous."
—Unknown

enjoy watching the Winter Olympics. Something about the white backdrop and the sports that this season's competition highlights is quite compelling. Maintaining strength, composure, power, and grace against the slippery nature of snow and ice is compelling to me.

Mostly, though, I like to watch the skating.

Over the past few years, I have come to enjoy skating and spending time on the ice. So, as I watch the athletes perform on that glassy surface, I truly, genuinely, appreciate their strength and ability. I mean, I am just content to skate around in a circle at a steady speed and not fall. The idea of the speed at which they move and the seemingly easy way they maintain composure and balance as they leap and spin even once, let alone three or four times, is mind-blowing. The thought of skating alongside a partner, jumping into their arms and trusting them to toss me about... all I can say is *WOW!* and *BRAVO!* Ice skaters are brave and beautiful.

My issue about this event—and many sporting events to be honest—is the commentary. I just want to watch them skate. I do not need to hear the accompanying critique about their "incomplete rotation." Obviously, I can see a fall when it happens, so I don't need to hear about that fall obliterating their medal chance. I do not require some "expert" to tell me about deductions and jump height. Every time someone ventures out on the ice—or up a snowy hill—I find myself holding my breath. I just hope for a clean, flawless performance. I cross my fingers. I hope they can bring their best performance to that moment. When they fall doing a trick or spin that they have probably done hundreds of times without error, my heart aches for them. But falls and mistakes and under-rotations happen... on the slopes and on the ice.

But I could really do without the endless critique against the music and pretty scenery.

I could mute the sound, I suppose. But I like the music and the sounds the cuts make by skates or skis when they meet ice and snow. That is a strangely peaceful sound to me.

Anyway, **Shut Up!** Let me watch and enjoy. Stop criticizing, pointing out flaws and imperfections. Stop analyzing or commenting on every move these individuals make. Enough of the judgment.

But wait. Don't we do that to ourselves? Think about this for a moment; how many conversations do you have with your Inner Voice? And... how many of those conversations involve your Inner Voice telling you all you have done wrong or what you have said wrong? How many of these conversations involve your Inner Voice identifying and brow beating you about some flaw, mistake, poor choice, or decision? And how often do you allow these comments to get to you?

Imagine for a moment your Inner Voice—that chatty commentator—sitting across from you at your favorite coffee shop. Create an image, body, and tone for your Inner Voice. Can you see it sitting there? Do you hear it talking to you? Is it a kind, supportive voice? Or is it hassling you? Be honest. Would you really be friends with this Inner Voice if it were actually a person? Would you even permit her (or him) to come in the door? What conversations do you have? Is your Inner Voice a cheerleader or a critic?

My Inner Voice has a lot to say. I hear about how I could stand to lose a few pounds. How I should not have eaten or drunk that. My Inner Voice tells me I lack talent when I don't get cast in a role at an audition or a call for an interview. She tells me how an outfit makes me look fat. She delivers criticism and reminds me of my flaws, unwise decisions, and weaknesses. She keeps me awake at night, nagging about this or that. Oh, it's all her opinion, but she has no problem sharing it. When I make a mistake, my Inner Voice tells me over and over what I should have done. She is kind of repetitive and corners me when I am vulnerable. My Inner Voice is a know-it-all... she is relentless and insists she knows what is best.

And believe it or not, I listen to her!

"We can make ourselves miserable, or we can make ourselves strong. The amount of effort is the same."
—Pema Chodron

During a yoga session when I am focused, calm, and peaceful, my Inner Voice breaches the quiet to criticize me when I fall out of a pose or cannot balance on one leg for 3 minutes... as if she could do any better. Well, she tells me she could... duh.

My Inner Voice has something to say when I pay bills or balance the checkbook. *Shouldn't have bought that,* she says. *Did you really need that sweater or new book? I mean, instead of a manicure or an updated kitchen, you could have saved that money and spent it more practically.* Oh, how I could improve my life if I would just listen to her!

My Inner Voice questions the way I deal with my kids and interact with friends. *Should not have said that. Should not have gone there. Should not have mentioned that. Should not have made that choice or decision. Why did you do that? Oh my gosh, I can't believe you wore that! You are weak for allowing that. You are a fool for believing that nonsense.* She debates my choices and my decisions. She challenges me at every turn.

Okay... my Inner Voice is kind of a bitch.

She is my own personal critic pointing out my falls and under-rotations. She analyzes and analyzes my choices (be they good or poor ones) and questions me at every turn. She is My Own Worst Enemy!

I try to mute her. I just want the nice music as I skate along. I just want to Roll with It, Baby, Breathe, and Let It Go. I want to find my Inner Angel and celebrate all that I am. I really try not to let her or her opinionated, know-it-all, critical voice dominate me. I often send her to her room and work on finding ways to shut her away. But she finds a key and a way back somehow and reminds me of my imperfections, challenging me when I am most vulnerable. At times I feel strong enough to ignore her. It is something I am working on. I am practicing mindfulness and studying ways to improve my meditation. I am learning new breath-work and finding more effective methods to stay present amidst whatever is happening to me or around. And I'm not inviting her to join me during that quiet time.

We all have our very own commentator inside us—our own worst enemy. And, if I am honest, I would not be friends with someone who talks to me, criticizes me, and abuses me the way she does. I would not meet her for coffee. Heck, I would unfriend her and block her.

So, each day, I seek to quiet her. I turn my focus to celebrating what I do well. I offer my best and try to silence the whisperings that seek to undermine me. I may fall on the ice—I may fall in a yoga pose. I may buy the wrong thing, do the wrong thing, or eat that extra French fry or two. But I remember in that moment, I am human, and I am offering up my best, and that every fall—or fry--gives me a chance to learn something.

And to get back up and try again.

On Beignets, Braces,
and Broken Noses

*"There is Hope after Despair.
And many Suns after Darkness."*
—Rumi

E nough is enough, right? How much can we take? Is it a challenge the Universe tosses out that suggests we need to find the answer to that question? Is asking for Patience the best way to find things thrown in our path that demand us to "find it within ourselves?" Well, that is the last time I ask for that!

There are times when Enough is actually too much. When you have had as much as you can stand. When the night is too dark. And the mood is too black. When anxiety rushes in.

Ever happen to you?

I'm quite sure most of us have had our own versions of "the darkest night." And I am probably correct when I say you might even have experienced a week, a month, or perhaps even a year of "the darkest night." In the crazy Covid-19 world, the darkest night seemed to be all of 2020!

What do you do to get through it? What are your crutches or methods to rise above... to claw to the surface?

In *Finding Nemo*, the good-hearted and optimistic regal blue tang, Dory, reminds the pessimistic and worry-wort Marlin to "Just Keep Swimming." No matter what happens— be it sharks or jellyfish stings or getting swallowed by a whale, Dory's sweet message comes through, " Just keep swimming."

But come on... she had short-term memory loss. She forgot if something bad happened anyway. Of course, *she* can stay positive.

In the Christmas classic *Santa Claus is Coming to Town*, the penguin, Topper, struggles with finding his footing and is reminded to "Put One Foot in Front of the Other." The penguin is obviously troubled. It belongs at the South Pole and is lost up at the North Pole. All alone. No family and completely disoriented. He's got his own issues. But somehow, Topper rises to the challenge and overcomes his troubles by surrounding himself with a new family.

Heck, even filmmaker George Lucas concurs, saying, "You simply have to put one foot in front of the other and keep going. Put blinders on and plow right ahead."

Guess he must have had some rough nights before *Star Wars* skyrocketed his career.

There are many Biblical quotes to help you through Dark Nights. Prayers and faith are a huge source of comfort for many, including me. Falling to our knees can be the best way to find comfort and strength. I have Bible verses bookmarked and sticky-noted on my computer screen to remind me that I am not separated from people who love me—no matter how alone I might feel at any given time.

I have my good days. My good months. My bad days. My bad months. I am probably just like you. It is the human condition to climb mountains and stumble into valleys.

Nothing makes the Darkest Nights go faster. But embedded in them is Hope. Hope that things will get better. Hope that *IF* you can shake off the fear and anxiety and stress—which in the grand scheme of the Universe are short term dramas—you will find yourself on the other side of the little black (or big black) raincloud. Over the Rainbow, if you will.

A few years ago, my son had an unfortunate meeting with a concrete sidewalk while in line for beignets at a local food truck rally. He passed out and face planted. It was a terrifying moment for me... and one where the calm of a mother truly set in. I was focused amidst all the blood (head wounds bleed a lot!), friendly with Ryan the Fire & Rescue Medic, and precise and appreciative with every doctor, intern, resident, and Emergency Room employee.

At 4:30 a.m. that night, though, the Darkest Night stirred and awoke me with a start, heart racing and anxious. I mean, all was well. He was okay, sleeping in the room across the hall from mine. But anxiety rose to the surface.

Yeah, I knew he would be fine. A little surgery the next week. Just a little anesthesia. A butter knife procedure to push his nose back into place, then another one a few months ahead to finish the task. But still...

My dramas are relatively small—in the grand scheme of things. There are so many challenges faced by the people surrounding us. But they are all significant to each of us... no matter how "small" they might seem to others. They loom large as we encounter them. And they invariably prompt "stuff," be it sadness, confusion, anxiety, stress, worry, emotion, outbursts, or tears of personal struggle.

People face health issues or lost jobs or struggle with paying bills. Covid-19 happened, and our world changed, forcing us to separate from others and wear masks. Racial injustice and lack of equality in civil rights resulted in protests with deep-seated anger taking over. People around us struggle with illnesses, face cancer with grace and strength, or deal with the death of a loved one. There is a lot of Stuff we have to deal with as humans every single day. And some days are just harder or darker than others.

My daughter—like her mother before her—needed braces. No big deal, you might say. But as I watched that little girl walk all by herself and climb into the orthodontist's big chair, I saw it as a rite of passage. In that moment, I noticed that my daughter—my sweet Angel Girl cuddling her not-so-stuffed bear Ba-Ba and mouse Squeaks in her arms—was no longer such a *little* girl. Was she ready to grow up? Was I ready for her to grow up? So much went through my mind that day as she began a dental process that lasted nearly seven years. In the instant she walked into that office, I felt the shift. It kept me awake as I worried about that transition and what it meant for her, for me, and for us many nights.

Like Topper and George Lucas, I will keep putting one foot in front of the other. Like Dory, I will just keep swimming. Sometimes though, I will shake. Sometimes I will cry. Sometimes I will rage at the sky.

When that happens... when the Darkest Night kicks in... I pray. I breathe deeply, sometimes even counting my breaths to find a sense of calm. I recall the strength I find on my yoga mat. And I am not afraid to reach out for help.

Sitting with Jarod at the top of Bridal Veil Falls in North Carolina.

"How can ye appreciate the beauty of the sunlight on the water if ye have not also known darkness."
—Kathryn Lynn Davis,
All We Hold Dear

During those Darkest Nights, I reach out to those with whom I am deeply connected. With an honest admission and plea for help, I receive the support I need to press forward. It is freely given. Calm seeps in after a while. Conversations with my dearest friends, my parents, and my brother and sister-in-law help me find my footing. A word, a text, an email, a Facebook message, a FaceTime Happy Hour, the touch of a hand or warm embrace, a smile, a thoughtful remembrance, a letter—these simple gifts offer me what I need to find some light.

Being held by someone who cares for me. Physical connection. Touch. My cat snuggling on my lap. My daughter reading beside me and reaching out one moment with gentle fingers to stroke my face and remind me that everything will be okay. My son stopping in to share a success moment or making me a pumpkin spice latte. My Faith. My Family and Friends. My Yoga. These are the things that see me through The Darkest Night.

Guess that's good, cause Jarod and I never did get one of those damn Beignets.

Use Your China

"Never put off for tomorrow, what you can do today."
—Thomas Jefferson

Last Saturday as I was cleaning the house for an evening with some good friends, I found myself looking at my china cabinet, wistfully. Several years ago, I purchased this Amish-crafted oak china cabinet after an especially stressful contract job. I had wanted it for an exceptionally long time, stopping in to visit it periodically on the furniture show-room floor. See, my mom had told me that once I had a china cabinet, she would give me her Aunt Grace's china. I did not register for china when I was married. I wanted Aunt Grace's set. As a girl, I had stood in front of my mom's china cabinet and admired it. The pattern was elegant... gold with black against a crème background. The salad plates were square. The bowls deep. And the gravy boat and platter were the most beautiful serving dishes I had ever seen. My mom had her own set, so we never used Aunt Grace's china. There it sat, collecting dust in Mom's dining room. Unused for decades.

When I finally acquired the cabinet, Mom brought it up to my house—triple-bubble wrapped—and helped me unpack it.

However, I have not used it much. Like it did under my mom's care... it was elegantly displayed, but left sitting quietly in the cabinet.

Not sure why that hit me recently. But as I was waxing floors and cleaning house in anticipation of guests for dinner, I found myself standing before my china cabinet just like I did as a young girl, wistfully gazing at something special and fragile. I thought about Aunt Grace.

What would she think of her dishes sitting on display like museum pieces? My discovery at that moment? I think she would prefer that they were used.

So, on impulse, I opened the glass doors and reverently removed what had long been kept sacred for "special occasions."

*Uncle Alba and Aunt Grace on
their Wedding Day*

I draped an elegant Victorian white tablecloth on the oak dinner table. I pulled out the chest holding my grandmother's silver— something else my mom had given to me, and I hadn't yet used. I selected cloth napkins, both my "Juliet" crystal and new "Scandal" wine glasses *(I figured there might be white AND red wine during the meal)*. I then took my time, dressing my table up with Aunt Grace's china. I laid out the salad forks and soup spoons, arranging glasses, dessert forks, and knives just like I learned in my eighth- grade home economics class. It was fun!

Sadly, I am fairly certain table setting for formal events is not taught anymore in schools.

When finished, I stood back to admire my creation, wondering why I had waited so long.

I never met Aunt Grace or her husband Uncle Alba. My mom used to visit their farm. She has many treasured memories of those visits. I learned very recently that she visited the farm for all of her special holiday gatherings. She showed me photos. But a small black and white photograph hand-sketched picture of Aunt Grace on her wedding day—and that china—is all I really know of a woman who played a pivotal role in my mother's early years.

I believe Uncle Alba was actually my Grandmother's uncle... making him my mother's great uncle and my great-great uncle. So, technically it would be my Great-Great Aunt Grace's china. Anyway... not sure it matters, except to tell me how old this Noritake set is. It's probably turn-of-the-century. It's numbered. It is registered. It is special. And I love it.

I like to think Aunt Grace loved it too. And that she would like to know that it continues to be treasured *AND* used.

So, on that Saturday night, I used it... I even used the tiny coffee cups and saucers, for my friend and I to indulge in an evening cup of caffeine as we enjoyed the sweet dessert my friend Cheryl made from scratch... Bubble Room Orange Cake. The recipe comes from a restaurant famous for its desserts in Sanibel, Florida. It was amazing. And I savored every bite.

Do you do that? Save things to be used only for "occasions?" Most people do. They choose to keep things under lock and key for times designated by our calendar as special or extraordinary.

My mom, Ellen Louise, as a child with her Uncle Alba and Aunt Grace

But it's not just "things" we keep under lock and key. It's not just things we keep hidden away for a special time. It's thoughts and ideas. Writings. Hidden novels and poems. Plans for trips. Emotions. Words. Aspirations and dreams.

Why do we not pay that complement? Why do we put off making that call? Why do we not make those plans with a friend we haven't seen in a while? Why do we wait and save our efforts for "special occasions?" What are we waiting for?

Didn't Harry Chapin's message get to you when he sang, "Cat's in the Cradle?"

We don't have any guarantees about tomorrow. Each of us plans and looks ahead as though we are promised a future. We ignore and dismiss today as we gaze longingly ahead... as we await the right moment or occasion. But what if we don't get that tomorrow? What if that friend moves away or that relationship fades into the background or the unexpected occurs? What if a pandemic should strike, and we can't see the people dearest to us—can't touch or get closer than 6 feet to our family or friends? What if you have left words unspoken and laughter unshared because you were saving them for just the right moment... for later... planning it for later putting it off until later.

None of us has any guarantees about "tomorrow." Oh, I'm not advocating behaving recklessly, or carelessly, or self-indulgently. But our founding father Thomas Jefferson knew what he was talking about when he said, "Never put off for tomorrow, what you can do today."

Yet we keep doing it. Saving things or conversations or plans for tomorrow. Refraining from reaching out or recognizing how much someone means to us until that "special occasion" comes along and all the planets align.

Consider this, from Proverbs 3 27-28, *"Do not withhold good from those who deserve it when it is in your power to act. Do not say to your neighbor, 'Come back later; I'll give it tomorrow when you now have it with you now."*

Bottom line... none of us knows how much time we have. Carpe Diem, a.k.a., seize the day. Make as many moments special as you can. Relationships are as fragile as Aunt Grace's china. Don't lock them away to pull out only occasionally when the "time is right." Don't hide your talents—or your ideas, thoughts, dreams, or words—under a bushel. Make the call. Start the blog. Search out a publisher. Speak your truth. Go on that dream vacation. Send the text. Make the time for that special friend. Reach out. Do not put off 'till tomorrow what you can do today...

And use your china.

Kindness in a Coffee Shop

*"Starbucks has a role and a meaningful relationship
with people that is not only about the coffee."*
—Howard Schultz

love Starbucks.

Of course, I realize that not everyone is a fan. Each of us have those coffee or tea shops that we gravitate to. But for me, there is magic inside Starbucks.

I suppose part of the appeal is the aroma of the beans grinding in those giant bins and the specialty coffees. The sounds and energy bustling around that place. The varied personalities working, meeting, reading a newspaper, talking, laughing, and making business decisions, as they sit together at tables or in the cozy chairs by the fire. So much seems to happen in coffee shops. Today, though, I found something that I was not expecting.

My absolute favorite drink in the world is Starbucks' Peppermint Mocha. I try to hold off until December 1st to treat myself to this high-caloric delicacy. But today's crisp air and wintery sky served as a catalyst, and I found myself donning hat, gloves, and my new winter white Olivia Pope wool "Gladiator" coat and walking to Starbucks.

My Olivia Pope "It's Handled" Coat
Photo by Dale Pegg

Walking in the door, I felt myself heave a great sigh as I took in the energy of Starbucks' highly caffeinated world. Wonder of wonders, there was no line. Must have been a sign from the Coffee Gods that this was where I was meant to be at that exact moment in time.

I glanced up at the vast menu, knowing what I genuinely wanted, and allowed myself to make the request.

"A Venti Peppermint Mocha, please." *(No wimpy Tall or Grande for me today. Nope. I needed the full rapture only available from their largest coffee.)*

The barista taking my order smiled. It surprised me. I needed that smile. It was a friendly smile, and I did a meditative action at that moment. I breathed it in. I absorbed the positive energy like it was a living spirit. And I found myself smiling back. It was as though his smile bestowed upon me a gentle touch that warmed me from the inside out. Welcoming. Encouraging.

Then he asked my name. They ask that these days and write it on your cup. I told him. Whenever I tell someone my name, they assume it ends in a Y. It's not a big thing. The majority of people spell it Jenny. And it's just going on a paper cup that I will throw away anyway, so I don't typically make a big deal about it. People misspell my name all the time, and I don't stress it. But the barista didn't stop there. He asked, "With a Y or IE?"

I was surprised. And I smiled again. "With an I," I told him. "And thank you for asking."

He grinned and laughed, explaining that he wanted to get it right. By his action, he honored my uniqueness—by simply writing out my name, correctly spelled, with black sharpie on the red Starbucks holiday cup. Then I tapped the scanner with my Starbucks app to ring up the astronomical cost for a Venti specialty coffee, which by now was even more worth it, and smiled again.

I moved to the waiting area. Others came in from the cold. Some smiling... some struggling with things I know nothing about. I found myself smiling at them. Sometimes people seem surprised when I smile at them—like I did—but often I see them brighten. We made casual chit-chat as we waited for our orders. A gentleman in a suit walked by me on his way out and complimented my coat. I smiled and thanked him, feeling stylish and happy that someone took the time, not only to notice but to speak kind words as well. He smiled back and exited into the cold. Our encounter ended.

> *"When we practice loving kindness and compassion,*
> *we are the first ones to profit."*
> —Rumi

The barista called my name and with great awe I collected my very first Peppermint Mocha of the season. I stepped back into the cold with lightness in my step. A little more ease between my shoulders. A gratitude that I found kindness today from strangers in a coffee shop. And that their simple generosity gave me something of great value. Something I guess I needed as much as I needed that Venti cup of coffee.

People need Gentleness and Kindness. Validation and Appreciation. Genuine Friendship. The Human Touch. They need a smile. These generous, genuine gifts we offer and receive from others ground and steady us, keeping us strong. Moving forward—no matter what else happens today—the smile from the barista and the words from the stranger will remind me that you can encounter and give Kindness anywhere. In one of my favorite movies, Walt Disney's live action *Cinderella*, the mantra "Have Courage and Be Kind" reminds me that by doing so, I can find the strength and resolve to make it through whatever comes my way. And, by sending Kindness back out into the world, I mindfully do the same for the people who cross my path.

When I smile at you, perhaps you will see the sparkly bright pink or soft aqua energy... my aura. There are days it's dimmer than others, but I seek to keep it pulsing with light. Perhaps you will breathe it in. Receive the energy I offer willingly. Sometimes, I run out, ya' know. So, when you share your Kindness with me, it sustains and strengthens me. It brightens my light.

What is it Blanche DuBois said in *A Streetcar Named Desire?*... "I've always depended on the kindness of strangers."

I am grateful that I can find Kindness in simple places like a coffee shop, from strangers. Sometimes it's easier to get it from someone you don't know. And to accept it. We like to project confidence. But there are moments...

That morning at Starbucks, as I glanced at rushed, harried faces, I realized the toll our day-to-day living takes. I observed and recognized that our spirits are fragile—especially at the Holiday time with the extra pressure, lists, demands, and emotional implications. Our pace in our daily existence, with its shifts and constant changes, challenge us. And it leaves us ragged at times. So much benefit can come from the simplicity of a smile. When I went to Starbucks that morning, I didn't know I would gain so much.

Dear Starbucks... Thank you for the Coffee. And thank you for the Kindness. I will see you soon.

Taking Child's Pose... *Inconceivable!*

Ego says: "Once everything falls into place, I will find peace."
Spirit says: "Find peace and everything will fall into place."
—Marianne Williamson

f I asked whether you have seen the 1987 Rob Reiner film *The Princess Bride*, I would predict quite a few of you would say "yes." I remember the very first time I saw that film. I rented it from a Blockbuster Video rental store and watched it multiple times. It is iconic.

For those of you who have seen this film, do you remember Vizzini? Do you remember what he repeated over and over when facing truths and rejecting them? Quite sure you must...

"Inconceivable."

Of course, he said it with the character's signature lisp, but the word echoes in my mind as clearly as the sound of his voice.

I thought of that the other day in my morning yoga session. We were invited to take Child's Pose at any time during the class. If things became too much or we needed something different, we are always given permission to "take Child's Pose." Whether you do yoga or not, that name might cause you to automatically assume it is a simple, quiet, less active place.

But for the first time—at that very moment—it hit me that Child's Pose is not necessarily a "quiet pose," after all, that what the instructor was asking me to do did not mean what I initially thought it meant. To borrow another Princess Bride phrase: *"Let me 'splain. No, there is too much... let me sum up."* In yoga, as in most exercise classes, you follow directions. Someone talks, guiding you into poses and through various flows. That is one of the things that I appreciate. During that hour, I can put down my Julie-McCoy- Cruise-Director clipboard and divest myself of the controlled, organized, in-charge, decision-making role. I am told what to do and where to move. I am prompted gently concerning the direction my mind should take. During that time, I let go and leave it to someone else to guide me where I need to be, staying present and in the moment.

That is nice. Really nice for a control-freak, type AAA organizer. During yoga class, I am released from the stresses that come from decision-making. I do not have to plan dinner, create a shopping list, tend to my kids, deal with work stuff, run through that conversation I had or plan to have with a friend and its potential implications, decide whether I will make that call or write that text, determine which show to audition for, manage the budget... well, you get the idea. During that hour, I do not have to make any decisions at all. I just follow the prompts and do what I am told.

In a way, you would say I am like a child... dutifully following the directions someone gives me. Like Steve Winwood advises, *"Roll with it, baby."* During yoga, I just go with the flow, and do what I am told. Child-like, right?

Um. *(And here is what I figured out, so pay attention now!)* **Not!** You see, as I reflected in class, children are not that simple. They do not just "do what they're told."

My daughter, despite every possible effort, refused to *EVER* drink from a bottle. My son, no matter how many times I beg, plead, instruct, cajole, or even speak emphatically, somehow leaves socks lying about and his dresser drawers wide open. Nope, doesn't close 'em. No idea why. But I cannot seem to affect change there. No matter what I say, there are times *(not always, but times)* that **Children Won't Listen!** They will not do what they are told. They will follow their own unique path and do it their way.

Back to the idea of Child's Pose... while, at first, I considered this "opting out" and doing a simpler stretch, that's not it at all. During yoga, that's Inconceivable because you are still working, growing, and evolving, even in that pose.

So again, Inigo Montoya's clever response to Vizzini's repeated remark... *"You keep using that word. I do not think it means what you think it means..."* is spot on. Child's Pose is not shutting down. But by modulating the guidance called out by the instructor and choosing to seek quiet peace within, I can a learn to take that peace off the mat. Child's Pose actually takes me deeper. It gives me a chance to reset, reflect, meditate, and get ready for what comes next in my own time. To find my breath and go deeper inside myself.

Pretty cool, those Ah-ha moments.

Children are ever busy with their questions and exploration, as well as their high-energy and amazing sense of wonder. They do things their way from an incredibly young age. Sometimes, like in the case of my daughter, a very, VERY, young age. Though you can guide, suggest, and offer parental wisdom, they will still make their own decisions, discoveries, and—inevitably—mistakes. They do not come with a pre-established, proofread, glossy set of instructions. And, even if you raise them identically, they will not follow the exact same development process. They are active participants in shaping every aspect of their lives and their achievements. Every decision or choice affects them. And each one is important as they become the individual they are meant to be.

So, then, it is Inconceivable to think that Child's Pose is *just* a still, quiet pose. It is Inconceivable to think that during yoga (or life for that matter) all I am doing is following a set of outlined, pre-established steps and instructions and that my poses—and understanding of the poses—are identical to everyone else in the room. Child's Pose doesn't mean stopping or checking out. I'm not inactive, I'm just slowing down to let the yoga continue to work in me.

> *"Om. Sometimes I have to remind myself: no one's love for me is more important than my own, and I don't need anyone to tell me "good job" or "you're on the right track." External validation, permission seeking, and approval is a thing of my wounded past. My precious heart is strong and clairvoyant and the middle woman between this human experience and the transmission prescription of archangels. Every breath dreams me more and more awake. I am me, and I am enough. Namaste. That's it."*
> —Thug Unicorn

Though I "go with the flow," the way I do it and reach a pose—as well as what I experience as I get there—is anything but inactive or simple. I am guided intuitively to reach inside myself and learn, grow, stretch, reach, celebrate, or... well, whatever it is that I need at that moment.

Taking Child's Pose is not opting out. It is instead a meditational, quieter pose that challenges us differently, like children, to reach deeper and explore aspects of our selves without movement to distract our thoughts or bodies.

Ever sit still for 5 minutes? That ain't easy. But that is taking Child's Pose. It is quiet, yes... and contemplative and explorative at the same time.

Taking a "simple" Child's Pose? Well, that's ***Inconceivable!***

Get Your Ticket for
The Happiness Express

*"I don't want normal and easy and simple. I want painful,
difficult, devastating, life-changing, extraordinary love."*
—Olivia Pope, *Scandal*

Got you, didn't I? Who among us does not want that *Happiness Ticket?* Who does not want to ride that ride?

Happiness is an elusive, much sought after tease. We race after it, using self-help books as road maps. We listen to speakers extrapolate guidelines and flow-charts. We talk to therapists, spiritual leaders, ministers, and priests as well as friends and loved ones about uncovering what makes us genuinely happy. We do crazy things to find that much-longed- for blissful state.

With so many people looking for happiness, you would think it would be easier to find. So why, then, does it seem to be so difficult to pin down? Under what rock does it hide? And—here is the kicker—should you find that Zen, Happy Place, what kind of deal with the devil do you have to make to stay there in Wonderland?

I have heard it said that "Happiness is a decision, not an occurrence." That it's something you choose. No matter what comes at you, you can decide whether to allow it to thwart your joy or strengthen your spirit. That *Finding Joy* is not the same as *Living in Joy*. I learn that in my yoga practice. No matter what pose I am faced with, or how difficult/easy it might be, I can determine how to react and manage the challenges it presents. I can choose my response. And I can take that decision off the mat every time I walk back into the world.

I have also read that there's more to life than "Being Happy." Ironically, the very pursuit of happiness can thwart it at every turn. When you chase after happiness by itself, it is elusive. It's actually a companion with other virtues, not a destination you reach or a commodity you obtain in and of itself. We should instead look for Meaning. Investing in something bigger than our own personal agenda gives us a chance to engage our highest strengths and talents and enact servant-leadership. But be careful, taking too much on can potentially produce depression, anxiety, and worry.

Taking care of others allows us to transcend ourselves and reach beyond the present moment to affect change and serve something more significant. Sometimes it involves self-sacrifice or denying oneself. As Dickens wrote in *A Tale of Two Cities* and Spock later quoted in Star Trek's *Wrath of Kahn*, "The needs of the many outweigh the needs of the few... or the one."

Seeking Happiness can sometimes be considered a shallow endeavor, prompting us to choose things that make us feel good, satisfy a need, or encourage us to explore selfish desires. We want less stress and more peace. We seek a calm ride instead of one riddled with bumps and challenges. We want our lives to matter, and we want to experience Joy along the way.

Is that too much to ask?

Money does not buy you Happiness or Joy. It may get you that outfit you want or that book, or that house, or the cool car, or the pretty lingerie, or the silver hoop earrings, or the new camera, or the trip to Scotland which will make you Happy for a time—especially if you go on the Outlander tour and happen to meet Sam Heughan! But I digress since even that encounter will not necessarily buy a continued *Happy, Happy, Joy, Joy.* Happiness just is not that easy. Neither is shaping your life into a more Meaningful existence.

> *"The key to being happy is knowing you have the*
> *power to choose what to accept and what to let go."*
> —Dodinsky

When we seek the Happy State, we intentionally avoid rougher waters that might rock the boat, but which could actually enhance our resiliency and transform us into better human beings. We resist, avoid, dislike, and even resent those things that require us to make sacrifices and keep us from that longed for *Blissful State* on the warm, sandy beach of life. We steer clear of projects, people, or things that might challenge us or cause stress. But when we seek a more meaningful existence, we serve others and experience Joy.

It's a cycle, truly. I want Meaning. I want Joy. I find Meaning. I find Joy. Yeah! Did it, right?

Nope. Here is how I figure it works. Joy is just one aspect of your ride on the train. It is always with you. Embrace it and recognize Joy might look different than you expected.

While you ride, you encounter special moments of necessary respite or growth—gifts to support your journey at a series of stations. These can offer moments of peace and rest, or especially dynamic joyful times. You drive through them during your journey, disembark for a bit. You even make longer stops at times and relish the many blissful benefits of that specific station. Then you climb back on the train and continue your journey in an effort to find Meaning, creating delicious memories and amazing adventures while you grow and make your life count. Your ride gives you a chance to meet and touch the lives of others... to do what you love to do... to laugh and cry... and encounter Wonderland on and off the train as you travel along.

Joy is not truly elusive. It is with us all the time. When bad things happen to me, and I am "unhappy," there are moments I still laugh. There are moments after a cry that I smile. There are moments of Joy in all sadness and struggle.

My brother Jeff is a runner. He trains and runs half-marathons. He's been training for several years now. They aren't easy. I've seen him finish a couple, and he's pretty worn out at the end. But there's also a glow and a sense of accomplishment in his expression. A *Happy State?* I don't know; I'm not a runner. But he keeps signing up for these half- marathons, suggesting to me there must be something good that happens during his run, a higher reason that he keeps at it.

Joy. We seek it. We find it. We settle in for a bit and bask in its warmth. Then we get up and keep moving, taking that glow with us. It empowers us to touch the lives of others as we are called to along the way, doing the things we love to do and making

My brother Jeff and sister-in-law Marcy after his chilly April Carmel Half-Marathon

the most of the other stuff that comes up, too. And we shine all the brighter for the tunnels or shadows we go through on the journey.

We each already have a ticket to ride the *Happiness Express*, but it requires us to complete the work we are meant to do to become what we are meant to be. Whatever that is. Wherever that is.

Only then will we stop our pursuit.

Words to Say

"We have two ears and one mouth, so that we can listen twice as much as we speak."
—Epictetus

There is a woman who stands outside the post office every day, collecting money for the local Animal Shelter. Rain, sun, snow, does not matter. She is there. She has something she believes in and stands outside, sharing her mission with anyone who cares to listen... or donate.

I walk by her a lot as I travel around town for work or to yoga or to shop or eat or whatever. I smile at her. I exchange a few words. I do not necessarily donate money as I walk by every time, but I do make eye contact and speak. I don't even know her name, but I recognize that she has something to say as she stands there, and I want to let her know I honor her stance.

I fondly recall a church service I attended several years ago led by a dear friend of mine. He was a retired minister— sadly, he passed away almost two years ago. But he was and will always be a mentor of mine. I would sit at his feet anytime I could and listen to him preach. I would gladly debate, discuss, and exchange perspectives... learning along the way. During the church service (it was a Methodist service by the way) he mentioned both Buddhism and Judaism, honoring the words those religions have to say in his own message. He always had an

Reverend Dick Cheatham, a Minister and dear family friend

amazing, reflective, accepting, and open mind. He always offered words to say that were worth hearing.

Many of us have words to say. I choose to write them down. My son tells his stories in films, while my daughter writes fiction. We see words all around us. Poems. Stories. Concepts. Quotes. Ideas. Songs. They have power and energy to connect or disconnect.

No. That is not exactly true. The words do not have the power. The way people hear and interpret and respond to the words *GIVES* them power. I know many people who write status updates or commentary on Facebook or other social media. Sometimes, their words result in people removing themselves from their mailing lists or un-friending them. Such a strange concept. The Constitution guarantees that everyone has freedom of speech— that guarantees them a right to express their thoughts.

Like the woman outside the post office, these are people who believe in a cause fiercely and demonstrate their thoughts in print, by taking a stance outside a building, collecting money, or raising awareness. Okay, there are some who use words more aggressively and get "in my face." I'm not such a big fan of their approach. I was always told you catch more flies with honey than vinegar and choose a gentler way to express my thoughts. But they have words to say, too. I just might opt to steer a little clear of them.

But then, with all the words flowing, do we listen? I have read that "We have two ears and one mouth, so that we can listen twice as much as we speak." (I never knew that is an actual statement made by Epictetus. I just thought it was a something my mom used to remind me.) But, if I am honest, I recognize that I am much better at speaking than listening. The other day, I was hanging out with a friend. He was speaking. Before I knew it, I cut him off. He smiled politely, nodded, and listened to what I said. Truly listened. I could see in his eyes that he was focused on my words and that gave me pause... that discovery made me look a little closer at myself. I need to become a better listener.

My daughter has told me more than a few times that I cut her off and that it bothers her. She gives me a look when I do. I realize what I've done too late. But I hear what she's saying and what she is telling me. I apologize. It's something I'm continuing to work on.

If people have words to say, they deserve to be heard, not cut off or interrupted. Not redirected. Not brushed aside or deleted. Not abused for the difference of their opinion. We will not always agree. Debates may ensue. But listening to each other shows a respect that seems to be neglected.

Ernest Hemingway stated "When people talk, listen completely. Most people never listen." That is such an interesting and sad thought. Better still is Stephen Covey's observation that "Most people do not listen with the intent to understand; they listen with the intent to reply."

Lauren Oliver, in her book *Delirium*, wrote "I've learned to get really good at this—say one thing when I'm thinking about something else, act like I'm listening when I'm not, pretend to be calm and happy when I'm really freaking out. It's one of the skills you perfect as you get older."

I can do that... smile and be thinking something else, talk on the phone while typing on my computer or my phone. But if I am doing that, then I am not present or holding space for the other person. I am not honoring the words they have to say. If I want people to honor mine, the least I can do is honor what they put out there. And I want to do more than just phone it in. I want to truly listen to understand the message they are doing their best to impart.

I guess I am discovering that I have selected the people who surround me for the intriguing people they are, for the uniqueness they offer, whether I agree with everything they say, believe in what they hold dear, or agree to disagree. Perhaps by honoring their thoughts and listening to what they have to say, I might become wiser through that experience. Listening is an attitude that comes from the heart...an authentic desire to share and connect with another human being.

Yes, I have Words to Say... but I want to hear the Words You Have to Say, too.

Whenever you are ready, I will be here to listen.

More Strolling & Less Scrolling

*"Almost everything will work again if you
unplug it for a few minutes, including you."*
—Anne Lamott

Are we too plugged in?

I ask this question earnestly. I sat in a coffee shop the other day and watched people on the sidewalk walking along with a companion, but not engaging with the other person. They were either texting or talking on their phone. And I found myself wondering: *are they truly "connected?"*

I see people sitting at a table in a bar or restaurant, seemingly enjoying a night out with a friend, friends, or significant other, but so many of them have their phones out, clearly checking Facebook, posting on Twitter, or texting some message to someone not in the room. I watch them and ponder: *Why come out at all, if you are going to just spend the evening interacting with a computer?* There seems to be so much going on around us, but no one is connecting to each other.

There are so many ways we believe we stay in touch with our friends, family, and colleagues... Facebook, Twitter, LinkedIn, Instagram, Messaging, Texting, Email, Snap Chat, etc. But the simple human touch seems to be dwindling in importance. I sit beside people in meetings. Someone is speaking while their "audience" is made up of people scrolling through their smart phones or clicking their tablet to read an email or to look at something else... something that must somehow be infinitely more important than what is happening in that business meeting.

As I watched a couple from my cozy coffee house seat, I could tell they were together. But their actions drew them apart... the need to be plugged in seems to be interfering with relationships. I thought the point of the cell phone was to keep us in touch with each other. But does it, truly?

With the tablets and cell phones come noise. So much noise surrounds us. It is difficult to find a quiet moment amidst this incessant buzz. It is exhausting... constantly being reachable or plugging in. But when you are talking on the phone, are you truly dedicating attention to the person on the other end? Or are you typing on a keyboard or doing something else which, inevitably, takes you away from what could be a "real" moment?

When was the last time you turned off the TV and sat companionably with a loved one in silence, reading a book or newspaper? No music. No cells. No Apple Watch or tablets. Maybe you talked about random things... things other than what they did at work or the kids' latest achievements? When was the last time you or your kids walked in the house and didn't immediately turn on the computer, scroll social media on your phone, play Wii or Xbox, or watch a TV show? When was the last time you enjoyed a silent night... maybe played a board game, pulled out a puzzle, tried a card game, or took a long walk for some family interaction? When was the last time you had just a few friends over to enjoy some nice, easy, casual conversation?

Last night I sat with a friend and talked. No cell phones. No texts. No Facebook messages. I did not Tweet my location or "check in" on Facebook.

Why the world needs to know where I am at any given moment really baffles me.

I sat and enjoyed the company of another person. Shared ideas... thoughts. Laughed. Debated stuff. Played a game of pool. Disagreed occasionally. It was easy and refreshing. Nothing electronic to interrupt or interfere with being in a genuine relationship. My words were not perfect... sometimes I stumbled over them and struggled to get my ideas clear. I could not edit, delete, or review the messages before I spoke. It was honest. It was real. It was flawed and imperfect. Yet it was a most natural thing. Just spending time... unplugged.

In theatre, we call it being "in relationship." That means you are in tune to another person. Focused on them. Actively involved with what they are saying in a give-and-take kind of way. By focusing outside of yourself, you become more aware of what is happening with that individual and more in tune with what is happening around you. You look them in the eyes and connect. You remember things they have told you... reflect on times you have shared. You remember comments they have made with others. It is settled. It is genuine. As Barbara Streisand said so eloquently, "People who need people are the luckiest people in the world."

For many years when my kids were growing up, we traveled to Traverse City, Michigan with another family. We spent hours sitting by the bay, staring at the view. At night, we drank wine, ate cheese and crackers, and watched the stars. Often, we were the only people outside. We knew others were there—could see the glow from their TVs. But we chose to talk and enjoy the moments together, watching for shooting stars and snuggling under blankets as it grew colder. Morning came, and I walked the beach, cup of coffee in hand, lucky enough many times to have my kids walk with me. It was my favorite week of the year.

"Being connected to everything has disconnected us from ourselves and the preciousness of this present moment."
—L.M. Browning

Yes, I need people. Yet, I want to unplug with them. I don't feel that electronics can replace true human interaction. I don't want to engage in a long conversation by texting or messaging. I don't want to log into Facebook to find out what my friends are doing and hope they have time to "chat." Call me greedy, but I want the real thing. The touch of a hand. The smile that goes all the way up to the eyes. The laughter that I can see and hear. I want someone sitting across from me or next to me sharing a moment. Listening to me stumble over what I have to say, a real conversation that has not been edited fifteen times in an email, post, or text. It does not have to be perfect. Relationships are messy. I like them that way. I want lunches, coffees, drinks, long walks, and random encounters with people I may not run into every day.

I prefer strolling to scrolling. With my head bowed too long over my phone, I might miss something. The best moments can be fleeting.

And as I stroll, I want our cell phones to take a break, resting quietly in a pocket or purse. Listening to and sharing with the person by my side should be all the plugging in that I need.

Taking Off the Training Wheels

"Being brave doesn't mean you aren't scared.
Being brave means you are scared, really scared,
badly scared, and you do the right thing anyway."
—Neil Gaiman

A few years ago, I embarked on a personal adventure. I took a trip with a friend. Not "just" a trip, but a trip out of the United States. A trip that required me to stop postponing the hassle and expense in updating my passport. A trip to a place I had not considered visiting before—Punta Cana in the Dominican Republic.

I will be the first to admit that I have led a rather sheltered life. Mexico is the only foreign country that has hosted me. Oh, and Canada. I'm pretty much a domestic traveler. So, when my friend suggested Punta Cana in the DR, my response was a resounding "Huh? What? Where?" Not a very enthusiastic one, at first. But then, the day she mentioned it to me was frigid, blowing, and snowing for my daughter's *Frozen*-themed birthday party. When she clarified it was a sunny place in the Caribbean—warm with a beach—I was all in.

I took care of the passport photo and completed the application. And then I called the post office to make the appointment necessary to earn the United States approval to leave the country. My passport arrived in my hands in record time, and I was good to go. Guess the U.S. was ready to enjoy a few quiet days without me. I packed light... shorts and t-shirts, bathing suits, sundresses, flip flops, suntan lotion, my iPod, and about five books.

Okay... kind of light.

We arrived in Punta Cana at about 9 p.m. It was pitch black. We climbed down the stairway onto the tarmac and took a tram to the receiving area, where we paid $10 to enter the country. We collected our luggage (well, I collected my new hot pink Guess suitcase, though my friend's luggage was "misplaced" for a bit... then delivered to our hotel later that evening, much to her relief) and we boarded a shuttle to our resort.

Now here is where it got real for me. I am an adventurous spirit. I like new experiences and places. I enjoy trying new things. Okay... wait... stop... reverse that...

I am going to make a confession here. I like to think of myself as adventurous. I like others to think of me as daring, creative and fearless. I want them to see me as brave. I can be that... some of the time. But... I need to admit to you... it does not always come naturally to me. I can very happily cling to the training wheels, hide in the corner and stay silent. I like it there. It feels safe.

But here I was... primed for the adventure of a lifetime. My heart was pounding in my chest as I boarded that shuttle, I truly had no idea what was in store for me next.

You see, sometimes I need to make a determined choice to force myself out of the safety of my comfort zone. I want to choose adventure, challenges, and opportunities that I might be tempted to shy away from. I have been known to take a few moments and give myself a little pep talk—sometimes out loud. And then I leap... or at least skip... on the stones.

I will admit I was a little nervous boarding this shuttle in the darkness and glad there were others from the good old U.S. of A. on board. I was in a foreign country and weary from the travel. But then I gazed out the window and discovered a multitude of stars surrounding me.

Stars are everywhere, I know. But these stars were different. The constellations were in different places that close to the equator. And in that darkness, they were so bright. I could not stop staring. I was like a kid in the candy shop, nose pressed against the window. They were brilliant. Unlike my home in metro Detroit, there are fewer lights to block them. So, they seemed huge and numerous, glittering in the deep, deep dark navy sky.

During the day, I explored the resort. I did yoga and aerobics on the beach. I watched the peacocks. I took walks on velvety, white sand. I floated in the salty azure blue sea, waves leaping over me... splashing, nurturing, and healing me with soft warmth. I tried new foods (mostly successfully), President beer, European style coffee, numerous mojitos, and various other "specialty drinks."

I napped. I read. I walked. I danced. I reached out and took every moment by the fist to make the most of these four days in the Dominican Republic. I was going to be Brave, darn it. I wasn't gonna miss a thing.

I did a good job in mastering the fear. My friend and I explored. That earns good marks, yes? But that was not quite enough. I had long dreamed of swimming with the dolphins. So, I took another deep breath and leapt, booking my trip.

On the day of the excursion, I boarded a bus with a Spanish speaking driver. I was the only person on that bus. Just me. I rode out through rural Punta Cana into the wild and "rustic" overgrown area that was known as Dolphin Island. I was the first one there... alone with

people from a culture I knew little to nothing about, who spoke a language I did not speak. Then others arrived... couples from other countries who kept commenting on how brave I was for undertaking this adventure all on my own.

> *"Our Fate lives within us. You only*
> *have to be Brave enough to see it."*
> —Merida, Walt Disney's Brave

When we rode the boat to the dolphin area, I laughed as the spray hit me. When the staff said, "swim out to the middle of the compound," I swam. When the staff said, "hold on tight," I held on. When the staff said, "reach out," I reached out. I snorkeled with reef sharks and stingrays too. Words cannot express the rush of emotions...

Excited and scared... thrilled and terrified... but overall... Bliss.

My time in Punta Cana was amazing. I blasted through the safety net of my traditional comfort zone. I believe to grow we must do that. To truly live, we must explore and challenge ourselves to experience life—all of it. We have to encourage ourselves to try new things. We have to know when it's time to take off the training wheels. We have to buy the ticket and take the bus even though

we might feel that pang of fear. We need to learn for ourselves when we should hold on—even though our heart is racing. We need to decide for ourselves when we should let go. Life brings so many beautiful gifts our way. I do not want to miss them because I am afraid of them... of the consequences... of the experience.

I see too many people spending their time anxious. They try to discover some secret knowledge to cue them in so they can meticulously plan every experience. They make lists of things to do and goals to meet. They have expectations... things need to happen their way and meet articulated timeframes. They need to know what is coming.

If I am honest, part of me is like that. It is safe. And I like safe. I like to look forward to things. I like plans and goals. But what I have realized recently, is that so many unexpected joys have come my way from moments that were not written in my planner. These joys, people, and experiences arise from surprise encounters and have given me some of the greatest times in my life so far.

But—and this is something I am only beginning to understand—the only way we will truly know joy is if we *Open Our Heart, Release the Fear, and Walk into the Unknown!*

My unknown was going to another country, climbing onto a bus all by myself. and going on an adventure to swim with the dolphins. What is your unknown? Your fear? Can you let it go? Can you open your heart to what might come instead of limiting yourself to a list? So much can be discovered when you take a few moments to just look out into the sky and notice the stars and allow, with your Open Heart, unexpected Bliss to come your way.

I don't know about you, but I don't want to miss out on life. I don't want to make choices because I'm afraid of getting hurt. Not that I'm suggesting we live carelessly or be cavalier about our safety. But I have decided to make the choice to embark on adventures when they present themselves. Oh, it may not always end well, and I may fall and scrap my knees bloody by removing the training wheels. That happened to me when my cousin Mike taught me to ride a two-wheeler once upon a time. But, as I recall, I chose to get back on the bike.

Yes, I have known disappointment and pain from opening my heart. And I am very sure I am not done with pain. But I don't just want to play it safe and, as a result, miss out on life-altering, dynamic, exciting moments. On my journey, I have known incredible highs. And I hope there are more highs to come.

I have decided that I would much rather risk those potential tumbles then spend my entire life with training wheels on my bike.

The Corner Bookstore

My best friend is the person who will
give me a book I have not read."
—Abraham Lincoln

I stood surrounded by words
embraced by spirits wishing to
share their tales... their
stories.
Immobile, hearing only my breath
amidst palpable silence.
The eerie quiet
somber... reflective
even.
No laughter or common chatter.
No coffee smell.
No voices heard.
The very lack of sound shrieking volumes.
I moved so very slowly...
as in a dream.
A nightmare of no awakening.
Fingers touching empty spaces
and caressing bindings of what remained.

And as I wandered my thoughts implored...
Would you have been a future friend?
A confidant of my imagination?
But no response came.
Memories were conjured to my mind,

of faces and moments past.
People... treasured seconds.
Eyes glancing up from an escalator...
Connections in the fiction aisle.
A Harry Potter night.
Moments seated on the floor
Words in colorful bindings all around
As we selected the right one.
Dances on the stage.
Stories. And more stories.
Ideas and thoughts.
Smiles and warmth. Treats and coffees...
But we were Out of Time ...
The moment past.
Warmth welled up behind my eyes
as I realized the finality.
Emotion surged.
Aching loneliness.
So very final.
A refuge... a shelter... a home.
Gone.
Rejected.
Condemned.
Unnecessary?

Echoes of what once was so noticeably clear
just as they had been.
I could hear the vibrations of voices...
words spoken...
Feel a touch... a hand... a caress...
See the smiles of yester time...
Everywhere...
But these were all just shadows now
as the feeling of betrayal surged.

Tears.

Loss.

Sadness.

In a place that had once given

such love... such hope... such promises

of a better tomorrow.

So many will miss the welcome.

The refuge given by the simplicity of words and pages.

From bindings and stories.

Shortsighted choices condemned you, my other home.

And now my shop around the corner is no more.

-April 4, 2014-

The Wrong Class?

*"You wanna run away, run away, and you say that it can't be so
You wanna look away, look away, but you stay 'cause it's all so close
When you stand up and hold out your hand In the face of what I
don't understand My reason to be brave."*
—Josh Groban, *Brave*

Last week I went to the wrong yoga class.

How, you may ask, could such a thing happen? How could there be a "wrong" yoga class?

Well, not all yoga classes are created equal, believe it or not. Since beginning my yoga journey, I have discovered the subtle differences in the classes offered. There are Fusion, Vinyasa, Yin, and Slow Flow classes held at Yoga Shelter. Every now and then, there are special workshops. Other studios offer different variations with different names. A friend of mine is devoted to her Bikram Yoga. So, no, not all yoga classes are created equal—they are all different, offering their own particular challenges.

So, there I was at the Thursday 5:45 p.m. class... stretching and setting my intention like I do before each session begins. I am not chatty before class. I get on my mat and look inward. But then the music started. The poses began. And I quickly realized this was not my Slow Flow Class... this was Vinyasa. I had never attended a Vinyasa session... I had been curious and considered it, but I had not yet accepted the challenge. Until that fateful Thursday night, that is. I truly had no idea what to expect.

It started with the stretching and short, faster movements. My thoughts began to race as I made the discovery. And I was faced with the question, *was I going to fish or cut bait?*

There is no judgment in a yoga class. So, I could have picked up my mat and walked out without anyone thinking less of me. But then, I thought about the "intention" I had set before the session began, and I decided to breathe and keep flowing.

For those of you familiar with yoga, you understand that classes typically begin with the instructor asking us to set an intention. When I first began yoga, I had no idea what that meant. I thought of yoga as simply a new variation of my exercise regime. But I quickly discovered that yoga provides the invitation to take you deeper... if you choose to embark on that journey. It's completely up to you. But you are invited to practice (notice I didn't say perfect!) a mind, body, and spiritual discipline. You get out of it whatever you choose. Find what you seek. You offer up your best... and that is always enough.

Well, as I prepared for the class that evening, my "intention" was to find a sense of calm in the presence of the craziness around me. I'd been kind of stressed out. So, I was seeking peace amidst emotion, steadiness when I felt my world quaking. I was looking for inner strength and the ability to rise above what seemed to be exceptionally difficult challenges at that moment in my life. To find a stronger, less volatile perspective as "life happened."

And believe it or not, that is what I found.

"Sometimes the wrong train takes you to the right station."—Yoon Seri

See, as I was flowing poses faster than I ever had and trying to find my way through each flow, I realized that I was not in the wrong class at all. I was exactly where I needed to be to achieve what I had hoped to achieve. I was finding my own sense of calm, while moving without a guide. I was sweating and smiling and centered and still breathing. Just me, the heat, the music, and the mat. I modulated if I needed to, discovering confidence in my choices, and I just kept breathing and doing my yoga.

If I had looked more carefully at the schedule, I would have selected the 7:15 p.m. class: the Slow Flow Class. But, on this night, the Universe guided me to instead find Calm in a new Challenge. To discover a Strength of Spirit immersed in the Unknown and Unexpected. I was seeking and actually finding Balance and Inner Poise while my spirit and body were shaking as they had never before shaken. In those early moments, as I pondered whether I could do this and then decided "Yes, I can," I found acceptance, even when I did not flow the moves exactly as stated. I found Strength inside. I chose to be Brave when a part of me considered running for the door.

And it was an exhilarating, amazing, self-actualizing experience.

I did not do the moves perfectly. I do not know if others did. I never look around during yoga. I am very introverted on the mat. But I found a sense of joy as I created my own flow at my own pace. At every moment, I knew that all I had to do was offer the best of myself. I embraced the notion that, in the storms of life, if I offer the best of myself, I could make it through. Just like I did that night.

Do you ever find yourself in the "wrong class?" Maybe, like me, you are not in the wrong place at all. Maybe you are exactly where you are supposed to be in order to achieve or discover something you otherwise might miss or pass right by.

The bigger question is not whether you are in what you deem as "the wrong place," but what you will do while you are there. Can you suspend expectation, inner judgment, and whatever holds you back from offering your best? Can you strip bare the facade and look deeper to embrace what the Universe wants to share with you? Can you look with your heart and cease wrestling with the reason in your head? Can you find the joy within discomfort? Can you hold on for a moment more?

Can the wrong place actually be the right place?

An Uncomfortable Life

"Do one thing every day that scares you."
—Eleanor Roosevelt

I see her pretty much every day, pushing her grocery cart around the streets where I live. It is not L.A. or New York City; it's just a mid-size Midwest town. In the summertime, her skin has a tan glow... but not a healthy one. It is hardened and sunburned. She pushes her cart down the sidewalk outside my office window. The wheels rattle as she goes by. I think she takes shelter at times behind my building.

During the long Michigan winter, she wears a thick down coat, but her skin still shows a ruddy glow, hardened by the colder temperatures. She is still pushing that grocery cart. It is full of bags.

I saw her at Taco Bell one day. She was quietly sitting at a window table eating a box of tacos. Her grocery cart sat outside the window, parked like a bike near the doorway.

I do not know her name. I have never spoken to her. She never makes eye contact when we pass each other. She did not look up from her meal that day as my son and I walked out. But I see her. And there is one thing I have noted... I have never witnessed one time where she has held up a sign or asked for money or support.

I find myself wondering what her story is. How did she come to live like this... pushing a grocery cart around the downtown area? Where does she go at night? Where does she go when it rains or snows? What does she eat? Where does the money come from? How does she survive day to day to day? Why is she alone, pushing a grocery cart?

I have no answers. And I must honestly admit that I have never stopped her as she walks past me. Never asked her name or offered to assist her. That bothers me. See, I thought about it that day in Taco Bell. But then I did nothing.

Since I have never seen her ask for assistance before, I do not want to insult her. Perhaps nothing "happened" to place her in these circumstances. Perhaps she has found some sense of realness or satisfaction in the simplicity of her existence. Perhaps she has chosen this life... a life that to me seems riddled with strife and hardship. An uncomfortable life.

Life is filled with choices every single day. We choose what to wear, what to eat, who to talk to, who to love, and who to reject. We choose our activities and our goals and our hopes and our friends. We even choose our enemies. We choose to keep learning and growing and living every single day. Or we choose to settle in, sit on the couch or recline in our easy chair, and watch the world move along.

We choose to protect our heart or open it up. We choose to explore new activities (like Pole Fit classes or paddle boarding). We choose to push ourselves. We sign up for a half-marathon, run daily, or visit the gym when it is still dark outside. We choose to audition for that role. We choose to apply for a new job. We reach out or walk away. We choose the things and people to invest in... and when to let go of those things or people that no longer serve us. Choices greet us every time we step outside our door. Heck, just stepping outside is a choice.

I don't know whether The Grocery Cart Lady chose the life she is living or if she became a victim of circumstances that I can't begin to comprehend. I have never faced a situation like that. But I do not see her huddled on a street corner. I see her moving along and making her way in the world, as sure as I hear the wheels turn on her cart.

I would like to help her. But since I do not know how, I choose to help others from meeting her uncomfortable fate. I have sponsored three different children through World Vision and donated to various support-focused organizations. I have volunteered and served food to the homeless. I have stopped my car at an exit ramp to give a few dollars and a lunch to someone whose sign said they were homeless and needed help. I have paid attention and offered a smile instead of ignoring those who walk past or near me. I have opened the envelopes requesting a few dollars for a Thanksgiving meal. Not tooting my horn or asking for thanks... just saying that I believe it is important to do what I can do to make a difference in the lives of people around me, even if they are people that I will truly never know.

I have a good life... an easy, privileged one by current standards. I do not need to worry where my next meal is coming from, and I do not push a grocery cart around town. I have a home and plenty of clothes and shoes. My children can participate in the activities they choose, and I have my own car to transport me around town and beyond. *HOWEVER*, I do not choose to settle down to a comfortable life either. I challenge myself, embracing new experiences and opportunities. I reach out to those I care for and leap oceans for them, whether or not they step over a damn puddle for me. That is just who I am.

I'm over 50, but I'm not done yet. There are still so many things I still want to do. There are books I want to read, plays I want to audition for and perform in, knitting projects I want to create, and trips to Scotland and Paris that I hope to take. The list goes on and on. There's still so much more to be experienced! Oh, I recognize that I have accomplished a great deal and have much to celebrate— my theatre resume is diverse and extensive, I have a career with two positions that challenges me, I'm healthy and in shape, I'm helping raise

My most recent theatre production, Rumors, with fellow cast members Maddie, Ashley and Rebekah and our director Jerry November 2019

two exceptional "kids"—a son who recently graduated from Wayne State and a 16-year-old daughter, both with unique talents who are shaping their own stories yet still sharing so much with me. *AND*, I will soon have published my very first book—a long held dream of mine! There's a lot to be said for those achievements.

But I'm not ready to rest on my laurels and say: *That's a Wrap*. I still have many, many more Dreams, Aspirations, and Hopes.

I don't think I am unique here. If we continue to see our lives as a work in progress... as though we are a lump of clay spinning on a potter's wheel awaiting the pounding, shaping, and fire before we are finished... we will live an uncomfortable life. We will get bruised. But we will also discover life lived to our fullest, most authentic potential!

Sometimes what we choose to do directs our path outside our fundamental comfort zone. Sometimes it stretches us. Sometimes it hurts. But it makes us stronger. A diamond only becomes brilliant after years in the dark under pressure. So too, choosing to continue to grow makes us vibrantly alive. We discover we have words to say... and we find chances to speak our truth!

When I die, I want my tombstone to read "She Loved Deeply *&* Lived Fully." That might mean some scraped knees along the way, but it also means adventure, curiosity, and exploration. Great love might bring great pain... but it is great, so I will deal. And I will have lived and embraced all life has to offer with two hands. Oh, it won't necessarily happen fearlessly, since sometimes I will be afraid. But it *WILL* happen with a passion that enables me to push past the limits fear might try to impose.

The Grocery Cart Lady haunts my thoughts. Maybe someday I will reach out and give her a Taco Bell gift card, purchased because I was thinking of her as I ate my comfort food there one lunch hour. I wonder about her story. Maybe someday I will ask.

I hope I will never live her version of an Uncomfortable Life. Yet I don't want my own life to ever become nestled too deeply in a softly cushioned chair either!

"It is not the easy or convenient life for which I search, but rather, life lived to the edge of all my possibility!"
—Mary Anne Radmacher-Hershey

I may never know how she came to be walking around town pushing that grocery cart. But I intend to learn something from her example. Life can be uncomfortable. Life can be tedious, and life can be hard.

Coming to terms with this idea presents an opportunity for me. No, I do not want to explore her life. But I pledge to honor my own quest as it beckons me. I vow to avoid the easy road, to steer clear of the unkind road, but not to fear the bumpy road. I pledge to be curious and strike out on an adventure to fully live this life I have been given. I pledge to pay attention to the plight of those around me—people who are not like me and might be living their own Uncomfortable Life based on the color of their skin, their religion, their self-identification, or even the places in which they live. I pledge to be present. To pay attention.

And if it gets Uncomfortable, well, I guess I will face those challenges along the way. I mean, no one said childbirth was easy or pain-free... but the end results are pretty, damn incredible.

Soften the Focus

"The reason we struggle with insecurity is because we compare our behind—the—scenes with everyone's highlight reel."
—Steven Furtick

D o you recall a day when things did not go right for you? Maybe you did not get the job after multiple interviews? Perhaps you lost out on a promotion or an opportunity you were excited about? Can you recall a gym class when you were one of the last to be picked for that elementary school team?

Or a day when things just did not go your way at work?

Or a yoga class when you were trying to gently move from Majorette pose to Airplane to King Dancer and you fell over?

What was your initial response?

Okay, I will go first. It was: *what is wrong with me?*

Ever do that? Ever think that? Something does not go your way and you immediately turn on the judgment meter and begin listing your inadequacies, mistakes, or faults?

A few months ago, I had a very rough day at work. I was as low as I could get, so I reached out to a friend to share some tears and wine and find some much-needed consolation. She pointed out something to me... something I had not accounted for in my self-flagellation. She told me to stop judging myself so harshly and give myself a break... to be Kinder to myself. And, as this was a year I was truly focused on Kindness, her remarks shed a light on something I had failed to consider.

In all these scenarios, something went awry. But my response was consistent. It was to point the finger at me and create a litany of my failings— because, clearly, I must be the problem. Clearly, I was not talented enough or clever enough or good enough. I needed to be fixed. I needed to be better.

Why do we do that? Take in the blame or the shame? Why do we consciously allow ourselves to feel "less" because of something that happens while we work, play, and try to exist among other people and situations? Why do we judge ourselves harshly when someone fails to value us as we want to be valued—or when we fall short of some goal or ideal that we have set for ourselves?

We need to Soften the Focus—especially in how we view ourselves. We need to offer ourselves some grace instead of harsh judgment.

We need a Cybil Shepherd approach to our-selves.

Those of you who recall the hit series *Moonlighting* (circa 1985—1989) know what I am referring to: the soft lens used for all of Cybil Shepherd's close up camera work. It blurred the lines, romanticized her look, and softened everything about her.

We need to offer ourselves that same Soft Focus—to honor what we bring and release the judgment when something does not go the way we had intended or expected it to go. We need to be our own cheerleader. Not everyone is lucky enough to have a friend like I did that day—a friend who reminded me to Soften the Focus and be Kinder to myself.

My Daddy and me, Easter, when I was four years old

When I was growing up, my parents were always there to serve as my own personal cheerleaders. They helped me celebrate each victory—large and small. They attended every play I performed in while I was in high school and even after graduation when I moved to Michigan and began doing community theatre—typically buying tickets to multiple performances! When I competed in high school golf meets, my dad showed up on the course after work and sometimes even on his lunch hour, in the sun or pouring rain. My mom proofread every English paper I wrote, talking with me about the ideas. And they came to help and support me in the early days after both of my kids were born. They were there for the highlight reels. But they were also there when I didn't get the role in the play, when my boyfriend broke up with me the evening of the Homecoming dance, when my friends and I got into squabbles, when I lost my job, and when life got messy, tedious, and bloody awful. They were there Softening the Focus and reminding me that who I am and what I offer to this world is enough.

They lifted me up when I was a little girl. And they continue to do so today. Parents just do that for their kids—even when they grow up. They've known me all my life and don't judge me harshly when I lose my way or struggle. So, why should I do that to myself?

One thing I continue to learn is that I am enough. And You are enough. No matter what else. That is my truth. There may be those who do not recognize our brilliance and there may be times when things do not go the way we had planned. But we need to offer ourselves grace, choose to find a way to let go, and move forward.

On the mat in my yoga-speak I would say, *Breathe in Compassion and Exhale to Release the Judgment.* And if I happen to wobble or fall over while moving from Warrior Three to Reverse Half Moon, well, I will just Breathe in some Compassion, laugh a little bit, dust myself off, and get back on my mat. It's just yoga. I need to put it in perspective.

It's just _____ *(fill in the blank)*. We need to put it in perspective. We need to offer ourselves a little credit. A little compassion.

It is our mind that creates the struggle. We seek perfection and accept no less.

> *"All the variety, all the charm, all the beauty of life is made up of light and shadow."*
> —Anna Karenina, Leo Tolstoy

On my yoga mat, I have discovered an important perspective. A pose is a pose. A day is a day. A win is a win, and a loss is a loss. Offer your best and let go of the rest. Put it in Perspective. Soften the Focus.

Now, if I can just learn to take that Compassion—the Yoga—with me off the mat. Wouldn't that be something!

The Four "C's" of Yoga

*"Yoga does not transform the way we see
things; it transforms the person who sees."*
—BKS Iyengar

S o here we are nearing the end. Here we slow down and stretch before
the final moments. The essays in this book highlight how I begin my
work *on the mat* and find my way to take what I discover there *off the
mat.* Each day, when I roll out my yoga mat, it's not just exercise and toning
my abs that I seek to accomplish. Rolling out my mat begins a very personal
emotional, physical, and spiritual journey.

There are various ways to practice yoga. I've mentioned a time or two that
I personally prefer Slow Flow, which is exactly what it sounds like. You slowly
move from one pose to another, building strength through a combination of
lengthy holds, and focused breathing patterns along the way. Lately, though, I
have become a little more adventurous and tried out Fusion, which combines
Slow Flow with some faster "flows" that you memorize and process on your
own. But mostly in yoga, I try to *Not* think or control, since that is one of my
personal challenges, and something I seek to leave off my mat.

One key message I have learned during this journey: yoga is so much more
than the poses. The point is not that we can bend down and touch our toes. No,
what is important is what we find—what we discover and learn—on our way
down there.

Yoga is more than exercise. Yoga has the potential to be a transformative
experience. Yoga teachers make suggestions, guiding your flow in and out of
poses. They invite you to set an Intention at the beginning of class. They help
direct your thoughts as well as your physical exercise. They present ideas as
you practice.

One class I recall, led by Brittney, introduced the three "Cs" of yoga. And, during the 60-minute session, she explained them. *Concentration, Consistency,* and *Cooperation.* You *Concentrate* to remain present, to prevent your mind from wandering, and to build focus. You practice *Consistently* to become stronger emotionally, mentally, and physically. And you *Cooperate* with your fellow yogis, adding your creative energy to the room and inspiring each other.

But for me, there are five Cs. Next comes finding *Calm.* In a difficult pose, I shake. Sometimes I even fall. Sometimes balancing is too difficult. There are times I just can't do a specific pose. Instead of becoming impatient though, I practice cultivating a *Calm* response, and that's something I seek to take from my mat into the world after class... a *Calm* reaction when stuff doesn't go my way, when I struggle, or when I tumble.

And next, I work on one of the most difficult things for me. The Fifth C... Relinquishing *Control.*

Ask anyone and they will tell you that I am a Control Freak. Surrendering control is terrifying. I mean, how can I be sure my son will finish that project if I don't check in? How can I tell if my daughter has studied and prepared for her test if I don't ask? How can I know the showers will get cleaned if I don't remind my husband? How can I be sure I will get invited out by a friend if I don't reach out first? How do I know what's going on if I don't ask? How do I know things will go the way I hope they will go if I don't take steps to make it happen?

See, Relinquishing Control is difficult thing for me. I'm sure Idina Menzel's famous tune is known to all. Well, it's my Theme Song. I have an Elsa credit card, a framed print from the Broadway musical *Frozen* on my bedroom wall, and three charms on my Pandora bracelet reminding me to "Let It Go."

I include songs in my Apple Music playlists focusing on Surrender. I use essential oils like Release to foster peace somewhere deep inside me that will finally allow me to do just that.

On my yoga mat is where I do a lot of my work. I meditate before class. And there, I remain calm and even learn to laugh a bit at myself when I fall out of balance. There, I am learning to Let It Go. There, if the pose doesn't go the way I had hoped, I can choose to remain calm. On my mat, I concentrate, practice consistently, and cooperatively share my light with the class. I remain centered and calm.

There may even be a sixth C to yoga. *Coming* Back. Repetition helps me integrate what I learn on my mat into my life.

Each time I roll up my mat, I am different. Remembering to take my yoga with me *Off the Mat* and make the most of the strength, calm, and flexibility I find while I am on it—well, I guess that's what brings me back to it time after time.

If I can move from Boat Pose to Low Boat during a hot, sweaty class, I know I can find that same strength when I walk out the door to help me through whatever lies beyond.

When I leave my mat... that's when the yoga truly begins. That's where my work on the mat helps me become more balanced, focused, compassionate, hopeful, and strong.

Savasana: Climb Ev'ry Mountain

"Climb every mountain. Ford every stream. Follow
every rainbow. 'Till you find your dream."
—Rodgers & Hammerstein's The Sound of Music

It's been over 22 years since I took my final spin on the mountain as Maria in the stage production of Rodgers & Hammerstein's *The Sound of Music*. I know many see it as a saccharine-sweet story, but for me, it was so much more than just a musical theatre experience.

I became extremely sick during the second performance weekend—a reaction to decongestants that left me dehydrated and unable to keep any food down. My husband when out of town that morning with some friends for the day, so I was alone at home when I realized something was terribly wrong. Mind you, this was *before* everyone had a cell phone. I felt very isolated and scared.

I knew I had to get to the theatre for the show, but I couldn't drive. I felt weak and couldn't keep food down. (Wondering if I shouldn't, or wouldn't, be able to perform never crossed my mind!) I phoned a friend and told him what was going on. He realized that the situation was more serious than just a carpool. So, he phoned a couple doctors. Long story short—I know, too late—I was in the ER receiving two bags of saline.

We were less than four hours before curtain.

It was one of the craziest times of my life, laying there—my friend Joe looking sorta pale. I mean, I was the *LEAD* in this production that had been months in the works. And I was in an ER hospital bed with a needle in my arm in an effort to get me rehydrated.

Ninety minutes from curtain, I was released from the hospital. Joe drove me the thirty minutes to the theatre, turning me over to his wife Kim to help with my costume, hair, and make-up. I recall being unable to apply my own mascara. The nuns were already dressed— and several were actually praying using their rosaries. The seven children looked nervous. And the Captain— also a doctor—took my pulse and cut the hospital band from my wrist minutes before the director called places.

But, as any theatre person knows, the show must go on. Adrenaline, and perhaps the nuns' prayers, kicked in. There was *NO WAY* I wasn't going out there on that stage. Three of the girls—Caitlin, who played Brigitta, Molly who played Gretl, and Maura who played an acolyte—took my hands and smiled. They believed in me.

I made it to the Mountain. I made it through the entire performance. Two numbers in, I was feeling fairly normal. I think it was the grape Pedialyte with all the electrolytes the Captain—a radiation oncologist—gave me in the final moments before I literally hit the stage. In my heart, I knew there were people

counting on me—not only fellow actors but an audience that needed to experience the magic of the story, the message in the music, and the production we had prepared. I wanted them to join me in climbing their own mountain to find their dream.

Molly, on the Captain's shoulder, looked back at me as we took our final places before "climbing the mountain." Her smile strengthened me in that moment. Caitlin held my hand—I know her grip was a little tighter that night. I remember her face as she smiled up at me and said, "I knew you could do it. I knew you'd be okay."

I didn't know that, honestly, when I headed out on that stage for my opening scene. But she did.

And sentimentality aside, the Labatt's Blue Light that Joe handed me in celebration when I walked off the stage that evening was a nice final touch!

I learned something invaluable in that experience. I learned the incredible power of love and friendship. And I learned the true power of resolve—of setting an "intention."

In high school, I had a poster on my wall with a message that served me that crazy night and serves me even today. It featured a ballerina in a long white flowing gown. The words were simple:

"If you can imagine it, you can achieve it.
If you can believe it, you can do it."
–William Arthur Ward

This quote has guided my path for as long as I can remember. It has served as a lighthouse when doubts or struggles have come my way. My husband and I have always told our kids, that if they believe in themselves, and they do the work, anything is possible. Balancing in Half Moon is never easy... neither is anything truly worth doing. They seem to get that.

At the end of a yoga class, you move into Savasana. Also called "corpse pose," Savasana is a resting pose where you dedicate a few moments for the transformation that began on the mat to actually settle in. Those final moments of class prepare you to take your yoga off the mat as you return to whatever waits outside the door. These important, quiet moments when all conversation ceases and the room is quiet, allow racing heartbeats to ebb and breathwork to return to normal rhythms. It's in that time of the class that whatever you experienced during the past hour—the ups and downs, challenges and flows, struggles, frustrations, revelations, and monkey-mind mutterings—settle into your mind, body, and spirit to begin the transformation. Quieting the mind in those minutes is on you and not any easier than the rest of class. But, Savasana offers a final moment of peace before you return to the real world.

Since I climbed Maria's mountain back in 1999, I've ventured up and down many mountains of my own. I've dwelt in some dark valleys, meandered by gentle streams, rested by busy oceans, and shouted from the heights of both the Blue Ridge and Smokey Mountains. Along the way, I've relished the support of family, friends, mentors, guides, and a sweet cat. All in all, they played and continue to play an incredibly significant role in my journey. In many cases, they have no idea the impact they have had on my climb. And, in turn, I may never know the impact I had on theirs.

Bottom line, though, I come to my mat to do the work. And when I invest the time, energy, focus, and emotion into that work, I find the mountaintop. Well, maybe I don't find it every single time. But *I DO* find the strength, inner resolve, curiosity, and hope necessary to continue my journey.

The words of a Miley Cyrus song have become a regular mantra for me. They remind me:

There's always gonna, be another mountain.
Always gonna want to make it move. Always gonna be an uphill battle.
Sometimes I'm gonna have to lose. Ain't about how fast I get there.
Ain't about what's waiting on the other side.
*It's **The Climb.***

On my mat, I begin the climb. I reach the mountain top some days. On others, well, I'm still working through "stuff." But in those final moments of Savasana—no matter what has taken place during the last 57 minutes of class—I just breathe and allow the yoga to settle in. I can then find the strength to go back into the world, changed a little. Perhaps a little stronger. Perhaps a little more at ease with the slightly crazy, passionate, restless spirit that I am.

Then, I roll up my mat and walk out the door— different than when I walked in.

Then the work begins anew. Then, the yoga starts.

Paige, Doug, Jarod, and me hiking in the Smokey Mountains, August 2020

EPILOGUE

"You become what you believe."
—Oprah Winfrey

A t the beginning of this book, I talked about my early days in yoga and how they offered a new perspective on wellness. But those early days might have been short-lived, and I might have missed out on all the lessons yoga had to offer.

The very, very first yoga class I experienced—and I use that word intentionally—was that prenatal yoga program I mentioned earlier. Before the Dallas Cowboy Cheerleaders Yoga DVD and Yoga Shelter, there was Gaium's "New Method Pre & Post Natal Yoga" with Gurmukh Kaur Khalsa. I was 38 and pregnant with my daughter. My pre-pregnancy workout regime of weightlifting and aerobics was frowned upon by my doctor, so I needed a different option. He recommended prenatal yoga, and I agreed to give it a try. To be quite honest, I didn't want to give up my workouts during pregnancy. I was told anything you did regularly *before* you were pregnant you could continue to do *while* you were pregnant. And, well, I just didn't want anything to expand or shift too much to cause issues in the post-natal months.

Like I've said before... Vanity, thy name is Jenni.

I bought the video from Barnes & Noble. Yes, you read me correctly. At the time it was a *video*, not a DVD. I popped it in the VHS player, and I was greeted by a yogi name Gurmukh Kaur Khalsa, dressed in a flowing white ensemble and turban. She began the class with a chant in a language I had never heard before.

Sanskrit.

I learned *much* later in my yoga journey that this was fairly common. In fact, Sanskrit is the ancient language the first yogis spoke and the language in which many original, historic yogic texts were written. It is apparently believed to be a more potent language because of what is referred to as its "spiritual sound quality." If you listen when yoga instructors use it, the language possesses an almost sacred sound that is said to create sensations as well as vibration harmonies. Sanskrit is thought to actually connect students to the classical form of yoga that has been repeated orally for thousands of years. Each Sanskrit word is believed to have its own consciousness, and pronouncing the word allows you to tap into that consciousness.

I know, a lot of kooky sounding "wu wu." And that's exactly how I felt when I heard it the first time.

This was my very first yoga encounter. EVER! I'd done Pilates, yes. But before pregnancy, my exercise regime—which had begun with Jane Fonda at the age of 12—had evolved to numerous *Firm* workouts (from *Time-Life*) that integrated low-impact aerobics with 3, 5, 10, and 15-pound weights, a step, and a 20-pound barbell. The instructors sweat with you and cheer you on. Making it thru was the goal—and toned arms and jeans that fit were the incentives. Having no prior exposure to yoga, I have to admit that in those beginning moments I felt a little intimidated, kinda silly, and more than a little skeptical that this was going to offer any value for me.

I sat there in my basement, crisscross applesauce, feeling awkward as I followed along and began to explore the suggested poses. But after playing the video a couple times, something clearly clicked with me, and I kept coming back. Each time I played the tape and began to join in the mantra chants presented in those first and final moments, I found myself drawn in. Somehow the messaging and the movements helped me feel stronger, more capable, more powerful, and ready for what was eventually going to happen at the end of 9-months. I practiced daily and always looked forward to returning to my mat.

Unlike the workout tapes I'd done in the past, this prenatal yoga session somehow connected with my consciousness and inspired self-confidence, a sense of rightness in my body and mind, calm, and ease in my expanding body. Ultimately something about it must have resonated with more than my muscles since when the time came for Paige's official arrival in this world, I opted for natural childbirth.

Yep—me! I was the one who always said that when I delivered a baby there would be drugs to dull the pain. Lots of them. My preference had always been to go to sleep and have someone wake me and place the baby in my arms, all wrapped up, neat and tidy. I was all about a pampered birthing experience.

Something in the yoga messaging and the movements prepared me mentally and physically for the chosen drug-free delivery. Seriously. All I got was ice chips! I discovered on my mat that I didn't want to miss a moment of Paige's arrival. I learned how important it was to be present in my life—even during the hard times. I found inner strength, and I accepted how important it was to show up on my mat and take care of me. So, when the time arrived, I took that newfound confidence—along with my Josh Groban *Closer* CD, pillow, and suitcase—with me to Providence Hospital's Birthing Center.

That was the first time I took yoga off my mat. And in doing so, I experienced something unexpected, life-altering, and miraculous.

It took me a few years and an ugly struggle with anxiety to find my way back to my mat. But when I did, it was ready and waiting to support my work on regaining strength, calm, and balance—as well as develop tools to cultivate a healthier outlook and perspective. The messaging and the moves combine to do that with me.

However, it's not a race you win and quit. Even now, after over 10 years of yoga classes, there are still days where balance seems elusive and the mad monkeys chatter away in my mind in the 4 a.m. darkness. Breath and calm elude me. I get stressed. I am frustrated when I lose my balance or fall out of a pose. I get annoyed in traffic or dealing with to-do lists that are too lengthy. I struggle. I lose my temper.

Some days are just like that... even when you have all the tools in your toolbox.

But... *Yoga is a Practice.* It's not something you *perfect.* Some days you will fall out of a pose. Some days you may be distracted by outside "stuff." Some days the flows just won't really flow for you. Some days the most ridiculous things will get under your skin. Yet, yoga is something you can return to, knowing there's no judgment if you need to take a rest or alter a pose. I can offer myself compassion and remember that all I need to do is breathe. And, when I do that, the world seems to come back into focus, and I remember that I am strong enough to do hard things.

As I said in my opening pages, all we can do is offer our best and let go of the rest. I know firsthand that stars shine more brilliantly in the deep darkness. I've huddled in the dark and gazed at them up there, twinkling. We just do the work and then we let it go—in class and in life. On the mat and off of it. We are invited to choose in any moment to find ease, knowing that "After all, tomorrow is always another day!"—thank you, Scarlett O'Hara. And if we need to step out of a "pose" and take a breather, we can always begin again.

And again.

And again.

So, dear reader, I leave you with the message that Gurmukh Kaur Khalsa gave me on that prenatal video. The one that resonated so profoundly, inspired something buried deep inside me to grow strong and vibrant, and continues to guide my path as I roll up my mat and walk out the studio door time after time.

ONG NAMO GURU DEVE NAMO
Meaning: I bow to the infinite teacher within
and open myself to the infinite source of creativity within me.

SAT NAM
Meaning: This is my Truth.

ONG NAMO GURU DEV NAMO

I bow to the Creative Wisdom, I open myself to the Divine Teacher within.

This is my Truth.

SAT NAM

About the Author:
Jenni Carmichael Clark

Jenni Carmichael Clark began her yoga journey when pregnant to stay in shape. Inspired by the instructor and the teachings she learned from the program, Jenni gave birth drug-free and naturally in a birthing center—something she never would have anticipated.

When struggling with anxiety a few years later, a doctor suggested yoga and sent her back to her mat. As someone who regularly engaged in exercise to relieve stress, she recognized its value and gave yoga a second try. The result was life-changing for Jenni. She grew stronger through the poses and flows. But more importantly, she quickly found herself applying the teachings and principles presented in class to explore healthier ways to approach her personal well-being, mental health, and relationships. She left classes feeling not only better physically, but also calmer, more balanced, stronger, and more in-tune with herself mentally.

Jenni began writing about these experiences, sharing reflective essays in a blog called *My Own Little Corner by Jenni* (myownlittlecornerbyjenni.wordpress.com).

Jenni found clarity and grace on her yoga mat that she wanted to share. In this, her first book, she presents a collection of her thoughts, tied together with this theme. After over 30 years employed in the Communications and Event Planning field, Jenni's college English major—and decades of journaling and creative writing—aided her in compiling these essays.

Taking Yoga Off the Mat offers concepts that readers can implement to find balance, strength, and calm amidst their own day-to-day dramas. It contains ideas on which they can reflect and learn to take off their mat (real or proverbial) and into the world.

A Marketing and Communications professional who works with both a country club and professional theatre organization, Jenni also performs as a community theatre actress, loves to lose herself in a good book, explore waterways on her paddleboard, and knit. She resides in the Metro Detroit area along with her family—husband Doug, children Jarod and Paige, and cat Ellie.

Made in the USA
Monee, IL
07 July 2021